COUNTRY INNS
of *Texas*

CYNTHIA GRUVER

Photograph on cover: Located on Sealy in Galveston, this Queen Anne building was built in 1880 for Samuel Maas, a ship chandler, and his wife Isabella (sister of the composer Jacques Offenbach). The subsequent owner, Dr. W. C. Fisher sold the house to Cecilia Matali, wife of Amadeo Alabart Matali, a local building and cement contractor whose name is stamped in many of the sidewalks in town. Dan Dyer and Jim Wellman bought the Matali place in 1983 and converted it into an inn with an authentic Victorian atmosphere.

For more information about staying at the Matali see the review that appears on page 129.

Photographer: Gary Faye

PUBLISHER
Robert J. Dolezal

EDITORIAL DIRECTOR
Christine Robertson

PRODUCTION DIRECTOR
Ernie S. Tasaki

SYSTEM MANAGER
Katherine L. Parker

PROJECT COORDINATOR
Laurie A. Steele

MAP DESIGNER
Marti Walton Design

SERIES FORMAT DESIGN
Pentagram Design

PRODUCTION
Studio 165

PRINTING
W. A. Krueger Company

Library of Congress Catalog Card Number: 88-72349
ISBN: ISBN 0-89721-180-4

Published by 101 Productions and distributed by Ortho Information Services, Box 5047, San Ramon, CA 94583.

COUNTRY INNS *of Texas*

AUTHOR
Cynthia Gruver

ILLUSTRATOR
Roy Killeen

PROJECT DIRECTOR
Karin Shakery

PUBLISHED BY 101 PRODUCTIONS DISTRIBUTED BY ORTHO INFORMATION SERVICES

PREFACE

Texas is one of the most diverse and fascinating areas in America. The state is filled with a variety of landscapes, architecture, customs, food, and people, all woven into a multicultural flow of history.

To experience Texas fully, you must poke around on the back roads, for its charm lies in its small towns. Because of its sheer size, Texas is regionalized, and there is a strong sense of community. East Texas clings to the heritage of the Old South; along the border, the influence of Mexican culture is strongly felt (you might want to carry a Spanish-English dictionary when traveling here). German traditions dominate the small towns in the Hill Country, and hearty pioneer stock still tames the vast stretches of West Texas.

The scenery ranges from forests and lakes in East Texas to vast plains in the west. Like the landscape itself, the architecture covers an amazing range of styles. In East Texas, where you would expect to find vestiges of the antebellum South, you'll discover a surprising variety of Victorian mansions: Eastlake, Queen Anne, Steamboat Gothic. As early pioneers moved west, farther from civilization, the homes became simpler, often built of the stone, wood, and mud readily available on the frontier.

Amid this diversity, however, is unity. The focal point of each town is the courthouse. It is usually located on the main street in the center of the community, making it an ideal reference point when you're asking for directions. Often the courthouse is listed on the National Register of Historic Places or proudly displays a Texas Historical Medallion, granted by the state to buildings of historical or architectural significance.

During the six months I spent traveling around Texas, I found the state's country inns to be as diverse as their settings. Some offer a European charm, meticulously attending to a guest's every need. Others have a more casual, country atmosphere with furniture that is old and comfortable rather than antique. And, for a state that prides itself on having the biggest of everything, some of the finest inns in Texas are surprisingly small. The one constant I looked for was hospitality and charm, for if there is a phrase that characterizes the inns of Texas, it is "Southern hospitality." The innkeepers I met were warm and gregarious, going out of their way to make their guests feel at home.

Of the 180 inns I originally considered, only 56 are included in this book. If I felt uncomfortable or unwelcome at an inn, I did not include it. And although I prefer some of the inns over others, there are none listed here in which I would not enjoy staying.

This medallion is displayed on buildings of historical or architectural significance.

An added dimension to any stay in a Texas inn is that the innkeepers tend to be avid historians, proud of their heritage, proud to display it, and proud to share it. All Texans proved this during the 1986 Sesquicentennial when they invited the rest of the country to a year-long celebration in honor of their independence from Mexico, gained in 1836.

Don't hesitate to ask innkeepers what to do in the local area. You'll find they can recommend a wide variety of activities from trail rides to dinner on a riverboat. Like the other forty-nine states, Texas has its share of parks and scenic drives, museums and historic sites. For those who rarely travel without their golf clubs, most inns are located near courses; one inn even has its own. The eastern half of the state is dotted with lakes and streams offering all sorts of water sports, and the beaches along the Gulf Coast are some of the best in the country.

Antiquing is a favorite pastime in the Lone Star State, and half a dozen towns claim to be the Antiques Capital of Texas. Chambers of commerce provide guide maps to the antiques stores and descriptions of the types of antiques they offer, which range from trinkets to Eastlake Victorian bedroom suites.

Because of the abundance of magnificently preserved houses from the turn of the century, many chambers of commerce also provide information on self-guided walking or driving tours of the historic districts in their areas.

In the spring, visitors make a special pilgrimage to architectural landmarks; candlelight tours take place around Christmas. At these times, old mansions still being used as private residences are opened to the public. In towns like Jefferson, overnight accommodations are booked a year in advance for these events.

Much of the food served in Texas is good, plain country cooking, but don't overlook the justifiably famous Tex-Mex cuisine and the Gulf Coast shrimp. Texas restaurants also prepare some of the best continental cuisine I've tasted. But a word to the wise: Most inns listed in this book are in tiny towns that tend to roll up the sidewalks on Sunday afternoons, and many of the restaurants close. If you plan to stay over on a Sunday night, be sure to ask the innkeeper where, and when, to eat.

Texas is so vast and so rich in things to see and do that it should be savored a little at a time. Country inns make perfect base camps from which to explore. Each inn has something special about it, a personality formed over time by the love and care of its owners. This book is not meant to sit on a shelf, but to be used as a guide to experiencing the fascination of Texas. I hope each of you has the opportunity to enjoy the inns of Texas as much as I enjoyed researching them for you.

—*Cynthia Gruver*

RULES OF THE INN

Rates: Since quoting specific rates would make this book obsolete before it was printed, I have used the following scale as a general guideline: inexpensive, under $45; moderate, $45 to $75; expensive, $75 to $100; very expensive, over $100. An exception to this scale is made for the guest ranches, where the room rate usually includes three substantial meals, use of all the facilities, and trail rides. The scale for the guest ranches is: inexpensive, under $100; moderate, $100 to $125; expensive, $125 to $150; very expensive, over $150. All rates are for one night's lodging, based on double occupancy, and do not include tax.

Reservations, Deposits, Cancellations, and Refunds: Reservations are advised for all of the inns in this book, especially during peak travel periods. For holidays, weekends, and local festivals, the inns are often booked months in advance. Most inns require a deposit of at least one night's lodging, and some require a minimum stay of two nights on the weekends. In most cases, your deposit will not be refunded if you cancel at the last minute; sometimes even a week's notice is required, or a refund is given only if the room is re-rented. Call or write the inn in advance to ask about the current requirements, rates, and refund policy.

Late Arrivals: Most inns are too small to have a night staff, and since the innkeeper often must get up early to make coffee and cook breakfast, please try to schedule your arrival for late afternoon or early evening. If you are delayed, it is common courtesy to call and give the staff an idea of when you will arrive.

Housekeeping: In many of the smaller inns, guests share a community bathroom. Be sure to clean out your tub and washbasin, pick up your towels, and leave the bathroom the way you would like to find it. In many of these small places, the chambermaid is actually the innkeeper; keep your room as tidy as possible.

Tipping: In the larger inns, where you are presented with your check at the end of each meal, tip as you would in any hotel or restaurant. In the smaller inns, where the owner does the cooking and serving, you are not required to tip. In fact, most innkeepers will not accept tips, and some would be insulted if a guest tipped them. If you wish to express your appreciation, send flowers or leave some wine as you would in a friend's home. You should, however, compensate the innkeepers' helpers. Some inns have a "kitty" and divide the tips among the workers; others expect you to tip individually. I recommend that, at the end of a stay, you ask the innkeeper for advice on how to handle this.

No-smoking Policies: Many of the smaller inns do not allow smoking within the building, although in most cases guests are free to smoke outdoors or on porches, patios, or in the gardens. Others request that you not smoke at the breakfast table, and some of the larger inns have a no-smoking section in the restaurant. Inns have adopted this policy for important reasons: consideration of other guests and fear of fire or damage to priceless antiques. I have noted which inns have restrictions. Of those that permit smoking, many are not happy about heavy smokers, who can be annoying to other guests and leave the smell of their cigarettes in the rooms.

Pets: Very few inns allow pets, and those that do often have restrictions on size, or ask that you keep the animal outside in a dog run or garage. Others require a deposit. At those inns listed as allowing pets, it is wise to call or write for any specific regulations.

Wheelchair Access: Most of the inns are quite old and few are equipped for the handicapped. Several do, however, have ramps and ground-floor rooms. The innkeepers request that you give them advance notice so they can set up a wheelchair ramp.

Airport Shuttle Service: Shuttle service is provided by many of the inns located near airports. Usually there is a fee for this service, and in some instances it can be quite steep. Some cities, such as Houston, have a limousine service from the airport for a reasonable fee. Since many towns in Texas are fairly isolated, I have noted municipal airports for private aircraft. Most inns will be glad to pick up anyone flying a private plane to the local municipal airport as long as they have personnel available to make the trip.

Meeting Facilities: I have noted which inns have meeting facilities. Please bear in mind that these facilities accommodate anywhere from 10 to 350 persons. Always call or write and explain your specific needs well ahead of the meeting date to make sure the inn can handle your requirements.

Liquor Laws: Texas liquor laws are confusing. There are actually towns where you can buy a drink on one side of the street but not the other. In "dry" areas you cannot buy alcohol unless you join a private club, usually for a nominal fee. Restaurants in dry areas often provide setups for patrons who bring their own bottles. Inns located in dry areas that have bars or restaurants usually consider overnight guests automatic members of their private clubs. Many innkeepers do not object to guests bringing liquor for their own consumption. Some innkeepers even provide glasses and mixers. Inquire about the inn's policy concerning liquor when you reserve a room.

CONTENTS

WEST TEXAS

MARATHON
FORT DAVIS

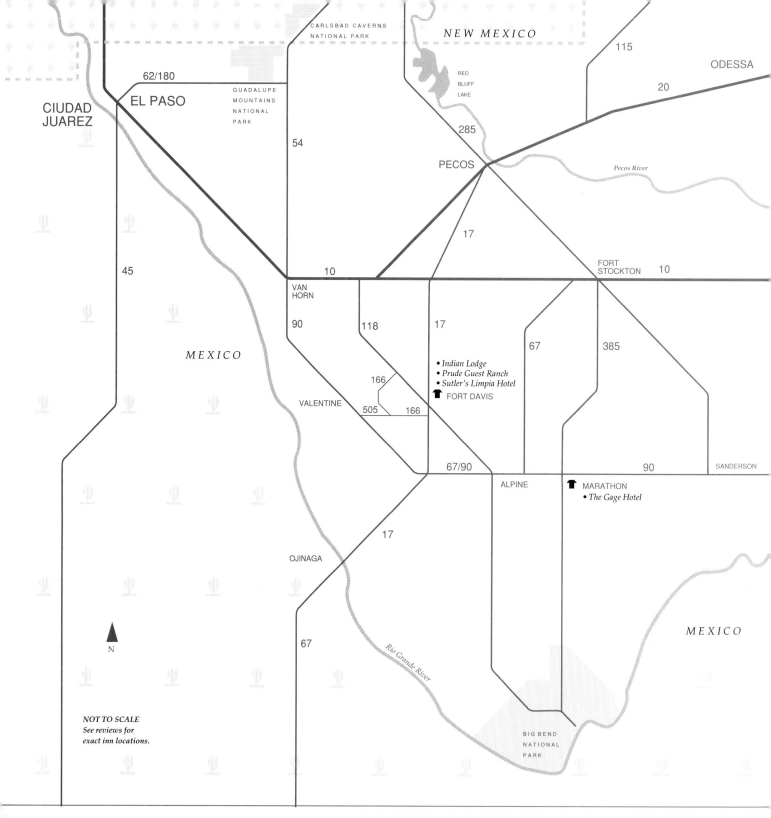

CARLSBAD CAVERNS
NATIONAL PARK

NEW MEXICO

ODESSA

115

20

RED
BLUFF
LAKE

62/180

EL PASO

GUADALUPE
MOUNTAINS
NATIONAL
PARK

CIUDAD
JUAREZ

54

285

Pecos River

PECOS

17

45

FORT
STOCKTON

10

10

VAN
HORN

90

118

17

67

385

MEXICO

166

• *Indian Lodge*
• *Prude Guest Ranch*
• *Sutler's Limpia Hotel*
  FORT DAVIS

VALENTINE

505

166

67/90

90

SANDERSON

ALPINE

MARATHON
• *The Gage Hotel*

17

OJINAGA

67

MEXICO

N

Rio Grande River

NOT TO SCALE
See reviews for
exact inn locations.

BIG BEND
NATIONAL
PARK

WEST TEXAS

West Texas is a land echoing with legends: Conquistadors. Apaches. MacKenzies Raiders. Judge Roy Bean. Pancho Villa.

When the Spanish came looking for gold in the sixteenth century, they called this land *despoblado*, the "unpeopled land." Coach roads were established in the 1800s, and the army built outposts like Fort Davis to protect the scattering of settlers and the mail coaches from attacks by Kiowa, Comanche, and Apache.

Today, this part of the state is referred to as the Trans-Pecos and the Big Bend Country, but the land itself has been little changed by time. Dust storms still blind your eyes. The majestic scenery still dazzles them.

These are the wide open spaces one associates with Texas, and they are still sparsely populated. Few roads cross the great cattle ranges, and there is room enough for two national parks: Big Bend and Guadalupe Mountains.

Although most of West Texas is dominated by the Great Chihuahuan Desert that spreads north from Mexico, there is a surprising abundance of wildlife, from roadrunners to golden eagles, from coyotes to antelope.

The Rio Grande, which separates Texas from Mexico for some 1,240 miles, still runs wild through the 1,500-foot sheer canyon walls in the Big Bend. Thousands of people come each year to take float trips through the various canyons here.

West Texas is the highest part of the state, with ninety mountain peaks above five thousand feet. Here, too, are caves covered with ancient Indian pictographs and oases once known only to the natives in places like Hueco Tanks (now a state park near El Paso) and Monahans Sandhills State Park, where fresh water can be found between the wind-sculpted dunes by scooping a trench in the sand.

El Paso del Norte—the Pass of the North—Texas' first non-native settlement, began as the village of Ysleta, an outgrowth of the Spanish mission relocated after the Pueblo Indians drove the Spanish from New Mexico in 1680. Today it is the largest city on the American-Mexican border.

Odessa is the hub of the Permian Basin, where a vast portion of the nation's crude oil, natural gas, and gas liquids are produced. Terlingua, in the Big Bend, is noted for its two annual chili cookoffs, both of which claim to be the official world championship.

Getting There: West Texas is most readily accessible by car or private plane. Amtrak stops at many of the smaller towns, and there are commercial airports at El Paso and Midland/Odessa.

Marathon is a tiny dot in the vast open ranch land of West Texas. The town, once the railhead for cattle ranches in the Big Bend area before it was overgrazed, still overlooks the main east-west rail line. Several times a day, containerized freight trains or the Amtrak express momentarily break the silence of the high plains.

Today, Marathon's claim to fame is as the "Gateway to the Big Bend National Park," the edge of which is only forty miles south. Hardly the place you'd expect to find a hotel like the Gage. It was built in 1927 by Alfred Gage, a banker from San Antonio, who at the time was one of the largest landholders in Texas, counting his land in square miles instead of acres. Alfred decided he needed a place to stay when he journeyed west to oversee his vast holdings. Since there was no comfortable hotel, he built one. He died the year after the hotel opened, but for years the Gage was the social, as well as the business, center of the area. Stories are told of the millions of dollars worth of cattle deals that took place in the lobby.

The hotel changed hands several times and eventually fell into disuse. Then, in 1982, the Gage was reopened by another West Texas rancher, J. P. Bryan, and his wife, Mary Jon. The Bryans, who live in Houston, spent three years restoring the old hotel. The original contractor was still in business in El Paso, so they were able to get a copy of the original blueprints and used them during the restoration.

Designed by Henry Trost, the two-story brick building is fronted with the architect's trademark, arched French doors. Though the exterior was sound, the interior had to be completely renovated. Woodwork was stripped, linoleum was removed from the pine floors, walls were replastered and repainted, and new plumbing, heating, and air-conditioning were added.

The hotel has been decorated with an eclectic selection of English and Mexican Colonial antiques and Indian artifacts. Yet the decor suits the setting. Under the high, beamed ceilings, the lobby is furnished with pigskin chairs and tables from Mexico. The original fireplace, which has never worked, is edged with tiles showing the brands registered by the first ten ranches in the area, including the one owned by J. P. Bryan's great-grandfather. On the mantle are a mastodon bone from northern Mexico and wooden ceremonial swords of the Tarahumara Indians, noted runners from the mountains of northern Mexico. A Peruvian leather trunk and Tarahumara and Tepuan baskets and pottery are also scattered about. The carved English cabinet is from the Gage Inn in England, and the long table, once used in the dining room, is covered with a Mexican weaving.

Just off the lobby is a bar that does not require membership. The pine bar is made from an old Mexican church altar, the wine rack once held the mail in a

THE GAGE HOTEL

Box 46,
Marathon, Texas 79842

Telephone: (915) 386-4205

Accommodations: twenty rooms with twin or double beds; private and shared baths with shower only; no telephones; no television.

Rates: inexpensive, no meals included. Restaurant open to the public for breakfast, lunch, and dinner in spring and fall, breakfast all year, and dinners on weekends during summer and winter. Children and pets welcome.

Cards: MC, V

Texas Medallion. Open all year.

nearby post office, and saddles from the late nineteenth century hang from the ceiling. During the tourist season there is live entertainment, but year round you'll find "chusa," an 1890s roulette-style game that hails from Chihuahua. The object is to roll the balls around the sloping circular table and bet on how many will fall into the brass cups at the center.

The guest rooms are spare (like the countryside) yet comfortable. Furnished simply with white cotton half-curtains, bare floors, and Mexican chairs, they are light and open. The beds, most of them custom made in the town of Alpine, sit high off the floor and are covered with woven Mexican blankets.

The nineteen rooms in the hotel are named for local attractions. Stillwell's Crossing has a nineteenth-century brass bed from France. The focal point of Persimmon Gap is a four-poster made in Nacogdoches circa 1847. Zane Grey stayed for a month in the room called Badlands while he wrote *West of the Pecos.*

The Gage's restaurant features the hearty food of the region: steaks, enchiladas, catfish, and a daily dinner special during the season. The dining room displays burden baskets, drying racks, pottery, and woven Mexican placemats. In the lobby you can browse through a scrapbook detailing each artifact in the hotel.

The busiest seasons for this corner of Texas are spring and fall, when the weather is on its best behavior. The hotel will arrange for horseback riding, pack trips into the Davis Mountains or Sierra del Carmen in northern Mexico, and float trips through Big Bend National Park. The Gage is also near Black Gap Wildlife Management Area and the Great Marathon Basin, a favorite with rock hounds.

Getting There: Marathon is about 200 miles east of El Paso on Highway 90. The Gage Hotel is on the west end of town. With advance notice, pickup is available at Amtrak or, for a fee, at the airport in Midland/Odessa.

FORT DAVIS

Before the trappers and settlers came west, before the California Gold Rush brought men by the hundreds, Apaches made their seasonal camps in the Davis Mountains. Volcanic in origin, these mountains rise from the high plains of West Texas to form the most extensive range in the Lone Star State.

From a distance, the mountains first appear as high mesas, edged with rim rock and seemingly as soft as moss. A closer look, however, reveals hillsides studded with rocks, juniper, and cactus. Farther into the mile-high range, the slopes are covered with oak, sumac, walnut, and acacia. In the valleys, pronghorn antelope graze side by side with cattle. Only power lines, stretching to the horizon, mar the view.

Though the Davis Mountains are situated on the northernmost edge of the Chihuahuan Desert, by their very height they catch the rain clouds and thus offer a green, cool oasis. Generations of Texans who could afford the trip have come here to escape the muggy summer heat of the cities.

But before the area was a tourist spot, the Davis Mountains were an important crossroads on the main El Paso–San Antonio road and the Butterfield Overland Stage Route. In 1854, to protect travelers and the mail coaches, the United States Army, under the direction of Secretary of War Jefferson Davis, built Fort Davis. The site chosen was Limpia Canyon, with its clear creek that would provide the camp with water.

The town of Fort Davis, like all small Texas towns, centers around the square, refurbished in the last twenty years. The old fort, which remained active until 1891, is located at the edge of town and since 1961 has been a National Historic Site.

The reconstructed barracks house a museum, open daily, that depicts life at Fort Davis in the mid- to late-1800s. A few of the houses on Officers Row have been furnished, and you can peek in the windows of the commanding officer's home to see how his family lived in this Wild West outpost. During the summer and on special occasions, park rangers and volunteers dress in period costume to give visitors a sense of history; the recorded sounds of a military retreat parade echo over the long-silent ruins.

Three miles north of town is Davis Mountains State Park, providing nature and hiking trails, camping and picnic areas. During the summer the park's interpretive center is open.

The seventy-four-mile scenic-loop drive that begins and ends in town is the highest and one of the prettiest roads in Texas. Along the loop is the Chihuahuan Desert Research Center, and at the top of Mount Locke is the McDonald Observatory, operated by the University of Texas. There are guided and self-guided tours of the observatory daily, and exhibits and slide shows at the visitors' center. The eighty-two-inch telescope is available to the public for stargazing on the last Wednesday of each month, weather permitting. Advance arrangements must be made by writing to the visitors' center at the McDonald Observatory.

In town is the Neill Museum, where more than three hundred antique dolls are on display, along with a dollhouse built in 1730. Big Bend National Park is some 100 miles south of Davis Mountains State Park, and Guadalupe Mountains National Park is about 120 miles to the northwest.

Getting There: Fort Davis is about 150 miles east of El Paso via Interstate 10, then 50 miles south on Highway 118.

After driving through the miles and miles of nothing but miles and miles that are West Texas, the Davis Mountains are indeed an oasis. Lush vegetation grows on the mountainsides and pristine streams trickle alongside the road. Davis Mountains State Park, which encompasses nearly two thousand acres, gives visitors a peek at the flora and fauna of both grasslands and woodlands. It is the only park that harbors the Montezuma quail, and during wet years the park is covered in wildflowers. Emory oak, gray oak, and one-seed juniper are intermingled with Apache plum, scarlet bouvardia, and other flowering shrubs.

In this setting sits the state-owned, pueblo-style Indian Lodge, built in stair-step fashion down the side of a hill. Most rooms face east and have a view of the sunrise over the park. The whitewashed stucco building stands out starkly against the rugged terrain and the landscaping of buckhorn cactus, yucca plants, prickly pears, ocotillos, and cedar.

The original lodge was built of adobe by the Civilian Conservation Corps in 1933, and then, as now, served as the primary lodging in the park. In 1967 a new wing was added, with twenty-four rooms, a swimming pool, and a restaurant. The new rooms are lighter, with larger windows, but have more of a motel aura, although the carved and painted furniture was made especially for the hotel.

The older rooms have a great deal of charm. Their eighteen-inch-thick adobe walls provide natural insulation, although all rooms in the lodge are air conditioned and heated, and the molded fireplaces are now only for show. Each room in the old section is different, with most of the furniture made by the CCC at the time the lodge was built. The Corps had its own sawmill, and the wood, mostly cedar, came from the area. The pieces are massive, each stamped and numbered and held together with wrought iron. The brown tones of the rooms are echoed in the *latillas* and *vigas* in the ceilings and the Indian motifs carried out in the carpets and drapes. Baths in both sections are modern, with tubs or tub/shower combinations.

The lobby, too, is filled with CCC furniture, and has a working fireplace. Whitewashed walls contrast with the dark wood of the beams and heavy tree-trunk posts that support the roof. The courtyard contains a small rose garden with a wishing well, and the balconies and verandas all along the east side of the lodge are filled with pots of flowers and cactus. There is also a telescope for public use.

Every year, on March 28, the barn swallows return to the lodge where they rear two sets of young before going back to Mexico in October. Under the eaves and patio ceilings are the mud nests, which often sprout curious birdlings.

Each of the four distinct seasons at the lodge attracts different types of people. In the summer, families come to hike in the mountains. In spring, when the

INDIAN LODGE

Davis Mountains State Park,
Box 786,
Fort Davis, Texas 79734

Telephone: (915) 426-3254

Accommodations: thirty-nine rooms with twin or double beds, king-size bed in honeymoon suite; private baths with tub or tub/shower; telephones; color television.

Rates: inexpensive, no meals included. Restaurant open to the public for breakfast, lunch, and dinner. Children welcome. No pets.

No credit cards.

Limited wheelchair access. Meeting facilities. Closed the two middle weeks of January.

17

cactus and wildflowers are in bloom, the birdwatchers come. Fall brings the senior citizens. And in winter, when this part of West Texas even gets a little snow, people come seeking peace and quiet.

Some regulars return every year to spend Christmas at the lodge, though that is the only day the dining room is closed. During the rest of the year, the dining room serves three meals a day, with dinners ranging from steak and lobster to Mexican food. The lodge allows guests to bring their own liquor as long as they do not drink in the dining room or in the public areas. Because the lodge has only thirty-nine rooms and is very popular, reservations are a must most of the year, and can be made up to a year in advance.

Getting There: From Fort Davis, go north on Highway 118 for 4 miles. Turn left into the Davis Mountains State Park. Once past the gate, bear to the right past the campsites. The lodge is on the hill off to the right.

In 1776, under the Articles of War, Congress granted certain concessions to the sutlers, the men who set up shop at army forts to sell their goods to the soldiers. There was to be only one sutler at each army fort, subject to army supervision. The sutler was required to pay a surcharge for every soldier at the fort, and to carry certain necessities in his store, such as clothing and groceries.

Many sutlers, however, abused their privileges, charging excessive interest rates or overcharging the soldiers without providing adequate services. As a result, Congress did not renew their licenses in 1866.

The army closed Fort Davis in 1891, but its little namesake town in the cool Davis Mountains began to attract tourists escaping the heat of summer. People stayed in the old fort buildings, and in 1912 a group of merchants realized the potential. They built a twelve-room hotel catering mostly to wealthy professionals, doctors, and lawyers. Built of native pink limestone, it was elegant for its day, with pressed-tin ceilings, gaslights, and oak furniture. They named it after the Limpia Creek on which the fort was built.

In 1920 another twelve rooms were added to the original building. But like many old hotels, the Limpia went through a period of change and then decline. It housed offices and a variety of businesses; the present small suite was once a doctor's office and the large suite a drugstore. The second floor became apartments for a time, and on the first floor were the administrative offices of Harvard University's School of Astronomy.

SUTLER'S LIMPIA HOTEL

Box 822,
Fort Davis, Texas 79734

Telephone: (915) 426-3237

Accommodations: nine rooms and two suites in hotel, eight rooms in annex, with double beds; private baths with tub/shower; no telephones; television in rooms.

Rates: inexpensive, no meals included. Children welcome. Pets allowed in one room in annex.

Cards: AE, MC, V

Limited wheelchair access. Open all year.

Sutler's Limpia Hotel

Renovation began as a class project in 1972, when school superintendent J. C. Duncan, who owned the building, had his students reconstruct a model of the town square as it would have looked at the beginning of the century.

The class project lead to the restoration of the hotel in 1973; the annex, which has an additional eight rooms, was renovated in 1983. Although the old sutler's store was between the hospital and Officers Row, not in the town, the Hotel Limpia has added the name to acknowledge the importance of these tradesmen to army life in isolated outposts.

The lobby has been decorated in reproduction Axminster carpets, flowered wallboard, and velvet chairs. The metal and milk-glass light fixtures carry on the Victorian theme. The front desk is made of oak and has stained-glass panels and a door from the Duncan ranch, built in 1894. The bulletin board is covered with articles and notes about the hotel and Fort Davis.

Two parlors open off the lobby, one with a television and twenty-four-hour coffee pot, the other serving as a living room, with a native-stone fireplace surrounded by comfortable Early American furniture. Beyond this second parlor, a porch runs the length of the hotel; it is now glassed in, and plants and rattan furniture surround oak tables large enough for a family game of cards.

Each of the two suites on the ground floor is like a small apartment with kitchen, bedroom, and sitting area. The small suite even has its own private screened porch. Upstairs, nine guest rooms are filled with reproduction oak furniture. Pressed-tin ceilings and transoms echo the past, while the private baths are modern. Long wooden valances hide the air-conditioning units, and the tall windows are draped with blue cotton curtains that match the bedspreads.

Tourists still come to Fort Davis during the summer, mainly from Texas and the neighboring states. There is little night life in town. The hotel is not fancy, and is showing signs of age here and there, but it does offer simple comforts and is an ideal place to escape the summer heat.

Temporary memberships in the restaurant next door are available. You can while away the evenings playing games and cards on the sun porch that overlooks the town square.

The Chihuahua Trail crossed the Butterfield Overland Stage Route at Fort Davis, and the longest stretch of the Butterfield Route still in use by horse and buggy goes right through town. Any afternoon you can take that buggy ride down to the fort and up the Overland Trail.

Getting There: Highway 118 runs through town; the hotel sits on the town square.

This ranch has been in the Prude family, in one form or another, since 1896. Once it encompassed most of the rugged land between Fort Davis and what is now McDonald Observatory—some thirty thousand acres. In the Crash of 1929, when the price of cattle fell from a hundred dollars to six dollars a head, the grandfather of present owner John Robert Prude lost all but the two-hundred-acre homestead.

Under the direction of John Robert's grandmother (who lived to be 101), the ranch became a boardinghouse for the men who built the road to the observatory. Word about her cooking soon got around, and people often lined up waiting to eat at Grandmother Prude's.

The business grew into a dude ranch in the 1940s, and for a while the two main attractions in the Davis Mountains were the Limpia Hotel and the Prude Ranch. John Robert took over the management of the ranch in the 1950s and eventually bought back 3,200 acres of the original land. As coach and principal of the local school, he was interested in kids and turned the ranch into a summer camp. It wasn't until 1983, however, that he realized parents needed a place to stay when they came to visit.

The Prudes were back in the dude-ranch business. Today four generations of Prudes help run the ranch under John Robert's direction. Most of the activity centers around the Big House, the original family home. Nearby are the stables, the heated indoor swimming pool, the rodeo grounds, and the 185-seat dining hall with Mexican tiled floors and ladderback chairs.

The food, served buffet style, is the good, hearty fare that Grandmother Prude would have cooked: chicken, roast beef, or steak, and at least three vegetables. The ranch cooks bake their own cobblers, cakes, donuts, and even hamburger buns. At the end of the enormous hall is an ornate bar with beveled mirrors from an old English pub. Though the ranch does not serve liquor, groups often bring their own bartender and bottles. John Robert bought the bar at an auction with plans to use it for wine tastings from the vineyard he hopes to plant one day. A meeting room beyond has a raised stage and is large enough for square dancing.

The guest rooms are also large, with heavy wooden furniture made in Mexico. All have tiled or wood floors and private baths, and some have fireplaces or wood-burning stoves. The family rooms have double beds and bunks, and bear names like Nut House, Spanish Room, Happy Place, and the End of Nowhere.

The more modern rooms are down by the creek, away from the center of the ranch. These are fourplex cabins with double beds and large baths. All these units have porches and rocking chairs where you can sit and enjoy the unobstructed

PRUDE GUEST RANCH

Box 1431,
Fort Davis, Texas 79734

Telephone: (915) 426-3347

Accommodations: fifty-six rooms with bunk, double, queen-, or king-size beds; some with wood-burning stoves; private baths with tub or tub/shower; no telephones; television in lodge and dining room.

Rates: inexpensive to moderate, breakfast, lunch, and dinner included. Dining hall open to the public. Children welcome. Pets allowed on leashes.

Cards: MC, V

Nonsmoking rooms available. Limited wheelchair access. Meeting facilities. Open all year.

views of the mountains and Limpia Creek. Some of these accommodations have windows on two sides so you don't even need the air-conditioning. Often the trail riders pass by, the horses' hooves splashing in the creek as they wind their way back to the stable, forming a picture out of the Old West. A hospitality suite at this end of the ranch provides meeting rooms, an exercise room, and a TV room.

Something is always going on at Prude Ranch. Part of it is still used as a summer camp where kids can join the ranch-hand program to learn the chores on a working ranch. There are English-Spanish workshops for children, and for adults square dancing, duplicate-bridge competitions, and art workshops. Nearby Sul Ross University attracts cowboys, so you just have to put out the word and you have a rodeo. There is also golf nearby.

The ranch's emphasis is on fun and old-fashioned companionship, and nowhere is this more evident than around the campfire after a cookout or hayride. At these special times, entertainment is more sedentary, perhaps listening to a lecture by a naturalist from the Chihuahuan Research Center or a storyteller's tales of fur traders. Some evenings, John Robert's father, John G., sings old cowboy songs. His knowledge is so extensive that the Library of Congress has recorded him singing some of the old ballads, including "Strawberry Roan," for which he is most famous.

The ranch's two-day package rate includes room and board. Most activities, like the trail rides and hay rides, are extra. There are no weekly package rates.

Most visitors to Prude Ranch are from Texas, but the rest of the country is also well represented, as is Australia, Britain, France, and Germany. There are special Christmas family vacations, though breakfast on Christmas morning is a little later than usual so John Robert can open presents with his grandkids.

Getting There: Prude Ranch is 6 miles north of Fort Davis on Highway 118. The large stone-and-wood entrance is on the right. Complimentary airport pickup available from municipal strips in Marfa and Alpine; charge for pickup at Midland/Odessa.

DALLAS FORT WORTH AREA

FORT WORTH
GRANBURY
STEPHENVILLE
GLEN ROSE
HILLSBORO

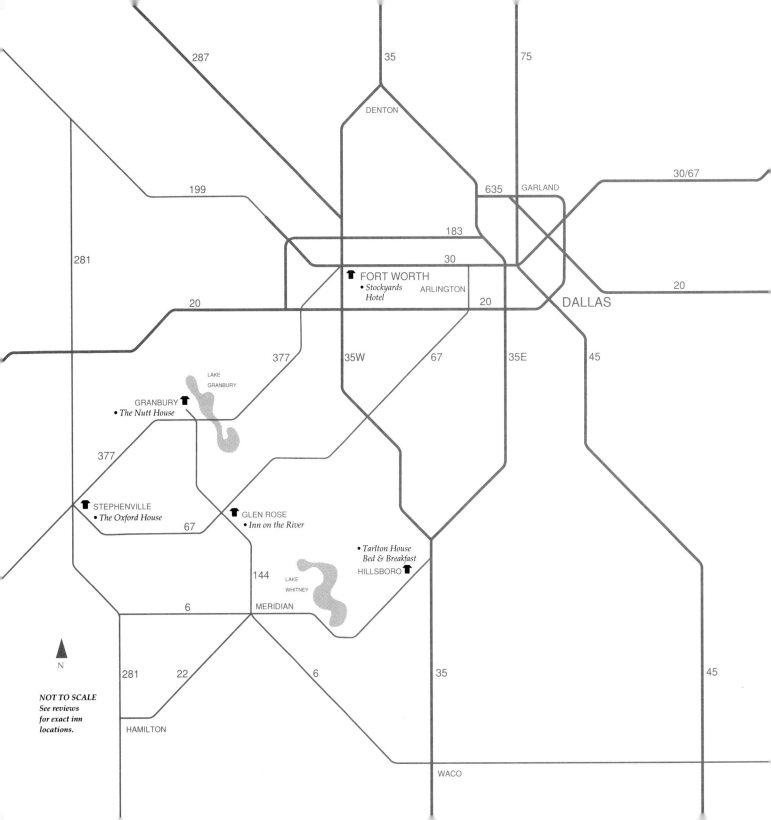

DALLAS/FORT WORTH

They call it the Metroplex, a sprawling complex that has grown out of the oil town of Dallas and the cow town of Fort Worth. Although freeways and suburbs string the two cities together, they remain distinctly different.

Dallas, the larger of the two, is a sophisticated, international city with men and women in three-piece suits. Here, it is said, is where the East ends. Fort Worth, where men still tip their Stetsons to the ladies, is where the West begins.

It is hard to imagine that the skyline of Dallas, today all glass and steel, began as a single log cabin alongside a ford in the Trinity River. Texas was still a young republic when John Neely Bryan built his trading post on the river. Freedom from Mexico had been won just a few years earlier, in 1836, and Texas would not be admitted as the twenty-eighth state of the Union until 1845.

The railroad came in 1886, and Dallas grew into a commercial center. But it was oil, discovered in the 1930s, that transformed the city. Wealth poured in, followed by the relocation of many companies from the North and the East. Fort Worth, just a few years younger than Dallas, also began along the banks of the Trinity River some forty miles to the west. As its name indicates, the town was originally a military post.

Established to protect the few settlers against Indian attacks, Fort Worth was named in honor of Major General William Jenkins Worth, head of the United States forces in Texas and New Mexico; on its site now stands the Tarrant County Courthouse. The Chisholm Trail passed through Fort Worth, bringing with it the great cattle drives and rowdy cowboys. Hell's Half Acre, with its saloons, dance halls, and gambling palaces, was once a hangout for Butch Cassidy and the Sundance Kid and a favorite watering hole for cowboys.

Shortly after the railroad came to Fort Worth, the stockyards were built north of town. Around 1902 two Chicago meatpackers, Swift and Armour, built plants here. The area, annexed to Fort Worth in 1922, became the biggest livestock market in the world. Ranchers came to the Exchange to trade beef and horses, and during World War I, a million-dollar-a-year business grew out of selling mules to the army.

But Fort Worth was not all cattle drives and gamblers. A local newspaper publisher named Stanley T. McBrayer invented offset printing there, too.

Both Dallas and Fort Worth have preserved their heritage. In Fort Worth, the Stockyards District has been restored to look like the Old West town it once was. Covered boardwalks, honkytonks, and chili parlors are bordered by a river walk. You can take a carriage ride through Sundance Square, with its red-brick streets, specialty stores, and art galleries, or see the longest miniature railroad in the country at Forest Park. Fort Worth has several outstanding art museums, a botanical garden, a zoological park, and live theater. Log Cabin Village preserves some of the earliest history of the area.

In Dallas, Old City Park, dedicated during the American Centennial of 1876, includes restored buildings depicting life in North Central Texas from 1840 to 1910. In the Swiss Avenue Historic District are some two hundred houses built in the early 1900s by the city's leading citizens. Union Station (circa 1916) is noted for its glazed terracotta walk and the vaulted ceiling in the waiting room.

The Warehouse District preserves the architecture of nineteenth-century industrial America, and the old brewery, built before Prohibition, houses restaurants, nightclubs, and offices. From the observation deck atop Reunion Tower, you can get a 360-degree view of the city. And just as one cannot visit London without seeing Harrods, you can't go to Dallas without spending at least a few hours at Neiman-Marcus in the heart of the business district. South of Dallas is Southfork Ranch where fans of the television series *Dallas* can tour the fictitious home of the infamous J. R. Ewing. The Texas Queen, an old-time stern-wheeler docked at Robertson Park, offers sightseeing and dinner cruises on Lake Ray Hubbard.

Getting There: Dallas/Fort Worth Airport is situated about halfway between the two cities. Airlines also fly into Love Field in Dallas.

Fort Worth, Texas. For many, these words conjure images of cowboys and Indians, longhorns and Cadillacs, oil men and cattle barons. The Stockyards Hotel delights in living up to this image. It is set smack dab in the middle of the Stockyards Historic District where Swift and Armour built their packing plants in the early 1900s.

This part of town, incorporated into the city of Fort Worth in 1913, was full of hotels during this time. In 1906 T. M. Thannisch, a leading businessman, designed and built the first brick building in the area, a three-story hotel that included a saloon, restaurant, doctor's office, and billiard parlor. Seven years later he built an addition; unfortunately, it wasn't until workmen joined the two buildings together that they realized the addition was eight inches higher than the original structure, an aberration that is just barely noticeable in some of the hallways.

For a time, the hotel was a home-away-from-home for cattlemen and their families. Then, after the last cattle drive in 1947, it went into decline. In the 1950s and 60s the whole area was depressed, and the hotel became a flophouse, its rooms

STOCKYARDS HOTEL

Main and Exchange, Box 4558, Fort Worth, Texas 76106

Telephone: (817) 625-6427 or (800) 423-8471

Accommodations: fifty-two rooms with double, queen-, or king-size beds; private baths with tub/shower; telephones; color television.

Rates: expensive to very expensive, no meals included. Restaurant open to the public. Children welcome. No pets.

Cards: AE, CB, DC, MC, V

Limited wheelchair access. Texas Medallion. Open all year.

Stockyards Hotel

renting for four dollars a night. About this time renovation began in the area, starting with Billy Bob's Honky Tonk.

The hotel's present owners purchased the building in the early 1980s and gutted it; only the facade is original. Rather than restoring the hotel, the owners remodeled it in what its management calls "period interpretation." The rooms are decorated in four general styles. The Victorian rooms, which overlook the three-story enclosed atrium at the center of the hotel, are furnished with white iron beds, fringed lampshades, and wicker chairs; the windows are covered in drapes and lace sheers. The Cowboy rooms, overlooking the Exchange, are done in a simpler decor with wooden shutters over the windows. The corner suite above Exchange and Main is where Bonnie and Clyde spent the night shortly before they were killed in 1933; the walls are lined with newspaper clippings and photographs of the duo, alongside Bonnie Parker's gun.

The Indian rooms are filled with Indian rugs, slate slabs for tables, and lamps made from Navajo amphoras. The Mountain Man rooms are large and oddly shaped. Since many mountain men were of Scottish or Irish descent, the corduroy bedspreads are edged in tartan plaid. Deerskins cover some of the headboards, and here, too, the windows have wooden shutters. The Celebrity Suite, suitable for J. R. himself, offers a hot tub on its own covered patio, a wet bar, and a working fireplace. All rooms contain soap, shampoo, a sewing kit, and rose-petal potpourri.

The baths have brass and porcelain fixtures and brass towel racks; some have claw-foot tubs. The oversized armoire in each room is made of handrubbed oak, as is all the furniture in the hotel. The handmade bedspreads are Brazilian, and the beds are triple sheeted. At night the staff will turn down your bed and leave you a copy of the "Cowboy's Prayer" and a sampling of Texas pralines. In addition, suites have remote-control television, wet bars, and small refrigerators.

The lobby is done in "cattle-baron baroque," with leather chesterfield sofas, Indian rugs, and replicas of wood-framed chairs carved with the longhorn emblem and covered in cowhide. One of the mirrors is framed with skins of white-tailed deer, and the walls are hung with original paintings. Bronze sculptures are set on pedestals of fossil-imprinted limestone from the Austin Chalk Fault. Also displayed is the saddle that once belonged to Pawnee Bill, who owned the first Wild West show before he sold it to Wild Bill Hickok. The pressed tin on the twelve-foot ceilings was reproduced from the original template found at the hotel, and the Axminster carpeting in the hallways was specially woven with a longhorn pattern.

The most unique feature of the hotel is Booger Red's Saloon, named for the famous bronc buster. Here bar stools are topped with silver-laden grand-entry saddles, work saddles, and even a sidesaddle for the ladies; the massive bar was made for the television miniseries *The Blue and the Gray* before finding a home at Booger Red's. The belt-driven fans, originally run by steam engine, are all on one pulley and circulate the air as they have since the hotel was built.

The adjoining restaurant offers an extensive wine list, though the most popular beverage by far is longneck beer. If you order beer through room service, it comes in a galvanized ice bucket. Also popular is steak and potatoes, and the kitchen makes cream gravy by the gallon. There is live entertainment Wednesday through Saturday evenings and Sunday afternoons. The once famous Lone Star Chili Parlor is now one of three executive meeting rooms that can accommodate 15 to 150 people. Also available for groups is the beer garden at the back of the hotel; this opens onto the river walk that meanders through the Stockyards District.

The District hosts two major annual festivals: Chisholm Trail Days in June and Pioneer Days in September. For these celebrations, streets are closed off and the sidewalks are lined with booths and food stands for a big block party. During the festivals Stockyards Hotel doubles its rates, yet is still booked a year in advance.

Getting There: The hotel is three miles from downtown Fort Worth and four miles from the convention center. From Dallas/Fort Worth Airport, take Highway 183 west to Interstate 35W south. Take the NE Twenty-eighth Street West exit and turn right. Go four stoplights to Main and turn left; turn left on Exchange. The hotel is on your left.

Most Texas towns have a central square dominated by the courthouse, which is invariably imposing and well preserved. In many cases the square remains a center of activity for the community. Granbury is no exception. The 1891 courthouse and several other structures of that era have been restored, and in 1973 the entire town square was put on the National Register of Historic Places. The square still bustles with activity. Tourists come from all over Texas and the neighboring states to see musicals and melodramas at the Granbury Opera House and to eat at The Nutt House.

Built in 1893 of handhewn stone, The Nutt House was originally a grocery store run by Jesse and Jacob Nutt; it was converted into a hotel about 1919. In 1970 the dining room was reopened by a direct descendant of the Nutts. Today it is renowned all over Texas as one of the best restaurants in the state, as the line of waiting diners that often winds through the hotel lobby and down the street attests. A noon buffet is served Tuesday through Sunday, and an evening buffet on Friday and Saturday. The food is simple, the kind prepared by the frontier women at the turn of the century. The menu rotates daily, and the meals are served family style

THE NUTT HOUSE

On the Square,
Granbury, Texas 76048

Telephone: (817) 573-5612

Accommodations: ten rooms in hotel, five in annex, with twin or double beds; one room has private bath, other nine share three bathrooms; five rooms in annex with private tub/shower; no telephones; no television.

Rates: inexpensive to expensive, no meals included. Restaurant open for dinner Friday and Saturday, lunch Tuesday through Sunday, closed from Christmas to early January. Children welcome. No pets.

Cards: AE, MC, V

Open all year.

at long tables; your tea, coffee, and soft drinks are brought to your table by wait-resses in old-fashioned dresses and white ruffled aprons.

The Sunday menu always offers a choice of chicken and dumplings, meat loaf, or ham. Saturday's menu features roast beef or baked chicken over rice. The daily buffet always includes four vegetables, a salad bar, and The Nutt House specialty, hot-water cornbread, no bigger than a three-dollar stack of fifty-cent pieces. For dessert there is a choice of peach cobbler or buttermilk pie.

From the tiny lobby with its plank floor, braided rugs, and church pews, a stairway leads to the ten guest rooms on the second floor. The parlor on the wide landing is furnished in antique wicker, and there is a pot of coffee brewing for the guests. Each room opens onto the landing, but only the front two have views of the square. Each has a ceiling fan and screen doors with half-curtains so the cool air from the central air-conditioning circulates. The rooms, with their high ceilings and tall windows, are furnished with iron or brass beds and oak dressers, some topped with marble. The furniture is a mixture of old and antique, and framed needlework decorates the walls. Only one room has a private bath; the other nine, each with a sink in the room, share three baths.

The hotel is beginning to show signs of age. The carpet is worn in places and the paint chipped here and there, but it is clean, comfortable, and somehow quaint.

Down the block and across the street is the Annex. In 1984 the former law of-fices on the second floor of this building were remodeled and turned into five guests rooms. Unless you prefer being close to the restaurant, consider staying in the Annex; the rooms are lighter and brighter than those in The Nutt House. Pale peach walls set off the oak wainscoting, doors, and window frames, and touches of peach are picked up in the country-print wallpaper and the tan-and-green carpets. The nine-foot windows are dressed with shutters on the lower part for privacy and with handmade lace curtains above to let in the light.

The floor was raised to accommodate new plumbing, so four of the rooms are split level. As in the main inn, older furniture is mixed with beautiful antiques, in-cluding iron or brass beds, wicker chairs, and oak dressers and armoires. Some of the antiques and the framed needlework are from the manager's personal collection. Four of the rooms are connected by the original double-transom doors, making them popular for family reunions. One suite also has a kitchenette.

The first settlers came to Granbury in the early 1850s, among them Elizabeth Crockett, who claimed land granted to her husband, Davy, by the Republic of Texas. One of the major tourist attractions in the area is Lake Granbury, created in the late 1960s by damming the Brazos River. Public excursions on the paddlewheeler

Granbury Queen run on Saturdays from spring through fall and on holidays. There is also fishing at Squaw Creek Reservoir, as well as beaches, a marina, and three eighteen-hole golf courses in the area.

In addition to the Opera House, Granbury has a Museum of Time with displays of antique clocks and watches. The visitors' center offers walking tours of the town, and at Christmas there's a candlelight tour of the historic homes.

Getting There: Granbury is about 40 miles from Fort Worth and 70 miles from Dallas. Highway 377 west takes you into Granbury town square. The Nutt House is on the right.

Toward the end of the last century, Texas lawyer and judge W. J. Oxford received a fee of $3,000 for legal services. He was paid in silver coins, and according to stories handed down by his son, W. J. Oxford, Jr., the old judge used those coins to build his house. In 1986 Bill Oxford, a third-generation attorney, and his wife, Paula, spent nearly fifty times that amount to restore the old family mansion to its original splendor.

W. J. Sr. built the house sometime before 1898 as a home for his wife, Elizabeth, and their children. After her death in 1904, he married again; a month after his second wedding, his new bride died from ptomaine poisoning.

The judge left Stephenville, renting out the house, first as a bank, and later as a boardinghouse for several Stephenville bachelors. A 1910 photo of the young boarders at the Oxford House, many of whom became prominent citizens of the town, was used as a model for the restoration.

In 1912 the judge married a third time. When he and his new wife, Myrtle, moved back to Stephenville in 1923, they began remodeling the mansion. They put a new hardwood floor on top of the old and removed the fireplaces and much of the fussy Victorian woodwork, both inside and out. French doors replaced the sliding doors between the downstairs rooms, and the tower, prominent in the 1910 photograph, was removed. They remained in the house until the judge's death in 1943. Myrtle, widowed a second time, lived in the house until her own death in 1983. During her later years, crippled with arthritis, she closed off the second floor.

After Myrtle's death, Paula and Bill went through the rooms, finding them crammed with mementoes of a long life. Many of the clothes and other items were donated to the town's historical museum, others to the drama department at the university. They also found old magazines, books, and an encyclopedia still unwrapped and in its original crate; these volumes now sit on a shelf in the library off the living room.

THE OXFORD HOUSE

563 North Graham,
Stephenville, Texas 76401

Telephone: (817) 965-6885
or 968-8171

Accommodations: four rooms with double or queen-size beds; private baths with tub; no telephones; no television.

Rates: moderate, Continental breakfast included. Children over ten welcome. No pets.

Cards: MC, V

Smoking allowed in parlor only. Open all year.

Many of the old mansions in Stephenville (including the home of the town's founder) are being torn down to make way for commercial buildings, but Bill considered it a matter of family pride to restore the house to the way he remembered it as a child. Judging from the photographs in Bill's scrapbook, this was a formidable task. The roof, which leaked badly, had to be replaced. The siding, patched over the years, was mismatched, so Bill salvaged siding from a turn-of-the-century house that was being torn down. All porches were rebuilt, and each spindle on the railing was handmade by craftsmen from a nearby Amish community.

The house has been refurnished with period pieces, some from estate sales and antiques shops, some family heirlooms, including the pump organ in the living room and the portraits hanging throughout the house. The tall windows have tie-back curtains, and some of the lace sheers are original to the house, as are the push-button light switches. Private baths were added to the four rooms upstairs, as well as individual air-conditioning and heating units.

The front room has an iron-and-brass queen-size bed—the only new bed in the house. The stained-glass panel in the front window, however, is original. The master bedroom, with its crocheted bedspreads and bay window, has a view of the courthouse where both W. J. Sr. and Jr. presided. The original bathroom is in a room furnished with a 1940s bedroom set that belonged to Bill's parents when they were first married. The rear suite combines an original bedroom and the maid's quarters at the top of the back stairs, which still lead to the kitchen. Paula has furnished this room with a sleigh bed and marble-topped side tables and dressers.

The fancy Continental breakfast is served on Myrtle's china with lace and embroidered tablecloths. Along with coffee, tea, and juice, the fare might consist of baked pears in wine or fresh fruit with poppy-seed dressing, homemade cinnamon rolls, or biscuits and sausage. Tuesday, Thursday, and Saturday afternoons the Oxfords serve a three-course high tea, and with advance reservations (and additional fee) they will arrange for an intimate candlelight dinner for two. The Oxford House will also cater luncheons and receptions for up to thirty people, by reservation only.

Stephenville is a quiet town. The inn is a place to come and curl up with a good book on the porch or on the small stone patio in the back garden, where the Oxfords occasionally serve homemade ice cream.

Getting There: Stephenville is about 80 miles from Dallas/Fort Worth Airport. Take Highway 377 south into Stephenville. At the stoplight, bear right onto Graham (there's a sign with an arrow that says Stephenville). The Oxford House is five blocks past the town square on the right-hand side of the road. Transportation available from municipal airport.

The Oxford House

len Rose was once renowned for its mineral waters, and as a result there were at least twenty sanitariums in town in the 1920s. Perhaps the best-known was the Snyder Sanitarium, built in 1919 by George P. Snyder. A man ahead of his time, "Dr." Snyder believed in drug-free treatments that included mineral baths, proper diet, chiropractic manipulations, and lots of relaxation. His reputation grew, and by 1927 he had added an annex. For forty years people came to cure their maladies beneath the three-hundred-year-old live oaks along the Paluxy River.

Relaxation is still very much a part of the Inn on the River. During the day, there are chairs for sunning by the swimming pool that overlooks the river, or for sitting in the shade of the live oaks that dominate the yard, while the staff provides amenities like a cooler of iced tea. The extensive gardens highlight any stay; rubber plants and ficus trees, ferns and succulents, flower beds and stone walkways edge the lawn. Frogs and cicadas fill the night with their chatter, the light of fireflies is reflected in the still waters of the river, and moonlight filters through the oak boughs that sweep the grass.

It's hard to imagine that this expanse of grass and orderly gardens looked like the jungle across the river when Steve and Peggy Allman bought the property in 1981. They had been searching for a country retreat for themselves when they stumbled across the old sanitarium, saw its potential, and bought it.

Renovation began on the annex, which was newer and more aesthetically pleasing, with gingerbread details on the front. The annex was seventy percent complete and already operating as a hotel when it was destroyed by fire.

It wasn't until 1984 that the Allmans restored the original 1919 building and opened it as the Inn on the River. When people heard the hotel was being restored, they sent old photographs and postcards, some showing their parents or grandparents (former Snyder patients) standing in front of the buildings. These pictures, along with those of the renovation process, hang in the two small library alcoves on either side of the lobby.

Today the clientele is mostly from the Metroplex, professionals who come to rest or to meet with friends. Small groups often rent the entire hotel for dinners and receptions or weddings on the lawn. The Allmans, who also own an interior design business, have filled the inn with antiques and reproductions, and reconfigured the original thirty-five rooms and nine baths into twenty-one rooms and three suites, each with a private bath.

INN ON THE RIVER

209 Barnard Street, Box 1417, Glen Rose, Texas 76043

Telephone: (817) 897-2101

Accommodations: twenty-one rooms and three suites with twin, double, or queen-size beds; private baths with shower and tub/shower; no telephones; no television.

Rates: expensive to very expensive, full breakfast included. Restaurant open for brunch on Saturday and Sunday by reservation. No children. No pets.

Cards: MC, V

No smoking. Closed Christmas Day and New Year's Day.

The original lobby with its twin staircases now boasts white-and-black tile floors, aqua grass-cloth wallpaper, and white beam ceilings. The wicker chairs are from Thailand, the hammered-steel chandelier once hung in the prestigious Fort Worth Club, and the reception desk and pedestal table were made from panels of the original door. Throughout the public areas hang quilts, most from estate sales.

Each guest room is unique. Twenty-seven different wallpaper patterns were used, and the beds were designed as the focal points: some antique, some reproductions, some custom made. Some are iron and brass with crocheted coverlets, some are wicker with quilts, some have custom-upholstered headboards and matching spreads. Venetian blinds fill the tall windows, a brass-and-white ceiling fan revolves overhead, prints and paintings hang on the walls, and each room has an antique wardrobe. The baths are all pristine white with ceramic wall tiles and faucets, oak fixtures, and beveled mirrors in brass frames. Some of the rooms are quite small, with only a daybed. The suites have sitting rooms with daybeds that can sleep an extra person. Two of the rooms open onto a porch with ceiling fans and lights for reading in the evening.

Breakfast and the occasional evening buffet are served in the Garden Gallery, a glassed-in dining area that faces the back gardens and the river. Breakfast is a hearty affair with such items as fruit in season, three-plum muffins, parsleyed cottage eggs, honey-ginger ham, applejack pancakes, and fresh-peach cheese blintzes. All the muffins and breads are home baked, the butters flavored with fruit. Off the dining area is a small, mirrored buffet area with round-the-clock coffee, tea, ice, muffins, and fruit.

Glen Rose is seventeen miles from the Granbury Opera House. Just outside of town are Dinosaur State Park and Fossil Rim Wildlife Park.

Getting There: From Fort Worth, take Highway 377 south to Granbury, then Highway 144 south to Glen Rose. Turn right onto Highway 67 into Glen Rose. At the stoplight, turn left onto FM 56 (Hereford Street), turn left again at Barnard. The inn is to your immediate right; the driveway to the parking lot is just beyond the building.

This blue-and-white Queen Anne Victorian with cranberry trim was built by Greene "Duke" Tarlton in 1895 for his wife and five children. Eight acres of vineyards, a large garden, stables, and small houses for the servants originally surrounded the house. It was the largest house in Hillsboro when it was built, and quickly became a landmark.

Tarlton, a real-estate lawyer, cotton farmer, and landowner, filled the house with amenities commensurate with his social position: a speaking tube to the second- and third-floor bedrooms, a dumbwaiter, and triple-hung window sashes. A spacious veranda curved around the front and one side of the house. The seven coal-burning fireplaces, each with an intricately hand-carved oak mantle, were inlaid with Italian tile trim.

Although Tarlton had owned land all over Texas and Oklahoma at one time, he died nearly broke on the day after his wife's death in 1931. The house remained in the family another ten years; then it sat vacant, labeled "the old haunted house" by the neighborhood children, and was eventually converted into a boardinghouse. It was finally purchased by Jean Rhodes and her husband, Rudy, whose family has lived in Hillsboro since the turn of the century. They restored the first two floors and opened the house as a B&B in 1985. Later they opened three more rooms, including a tower room, on the third floor.

The speaking tube no longer exists and the fireplaces were blocked off in the 1920s. But the 123 pieces of beveled glass still grace the front door, creating rainbows on the East Texas pine floors, and along the staircase five stained-glass windows remain.

The parlor is filled with law books and antiques. Seven-foot windows, trimmed with hayrack spindles, are shuttered against the hot sun. The fireplace is mirrored, as is the hearth in the dining room, which has lace curtains and the profusion of plants so close to the hearts of Victorians.

The second-floor guest rooms open onto a small landing-cum-library with bookshelves, couch, overstuffed chairs, and a tiny porch overlooking the front of the house. The Master Suite, also at the front of the house, has a bay window draped with lace curtains, a carved headboard, and a marble-topped dresser. The Sitting Room, which connects to the Master Suite by a sliding door, can be used as part of a suite or as a separate room. The private bath was once a second sitting porch and is almost as large as the room. Light and airy, the bath is dominated by a large claw-foot tub, the perfect spot for a long soak.

Among the other rooms is J. R.'s, with a forest-green-and-red plaid loveseat in front of the fireplace and a king-size bed. The French Room has a French armoire

TARLTON HOUSE BED AND BREAKFAST

211 North Pleasant Street, Hillsboro, Texas 76645

Telephone: (817) 582-7216 or (214) 821-0266

Accommodations: eight rooms with twin, double, queen-, or king-size beds; shared and private baths with tub/shower or shower; no telephones; black-and-white television in three rooms.

Rates: moderate to expensive, full breakfast included. Children over twelve welcome. No pets.

Cards: MC, V

No smoking inside the inn. Texas Medallion, National Register. Open all year.

Tarlton House Bed and Breakfast

and marble-topped dresser with a beveled mirror. The private bath is split level, with a shower on the lower level and a loft bed above, which makes this room popular with families.

The Rose Room on the third floor is one of the biggest in the house and overlooks the back gardens. The Paisley Room, as you might expect, is done in paisley, and the Tower Room is done in pastels. Although this is one of the smaller rooms, the four tower windows make it bright and cheerful.

The Rhodes' prepare special-occasion dinners or parties by reservation. Family-style dinners are available for bed-and-breakfast guests with advance notice and deposit. These are served at the long table in the dining room, looking out on the backyard, where breakfast is also served in the morning.

Two lakes in the area offer fishing, water skiing, and swimming. In June, the Chamber of Commerce sponsors a walking tour of some of Hillsboro's historic houses. Nearby is the Hill College Civil War Museum and Research Center.

Getting There: Hillsboro is 60 miles south of Dallas/Fort Worth Airport. Take Interstate 35W south to Highway 77, which leads into town. Turn left at the stoplight (Franklin). Go two blocks to Pleasant and turn left. Tarlton House is the third house on the left.

EAST TEXAS

BIG SANDY

PALESTINE

RUSK

JEFFERSON

NAVASOTA

BELLVILLE

CHAPPELL HILL

WEIMAR

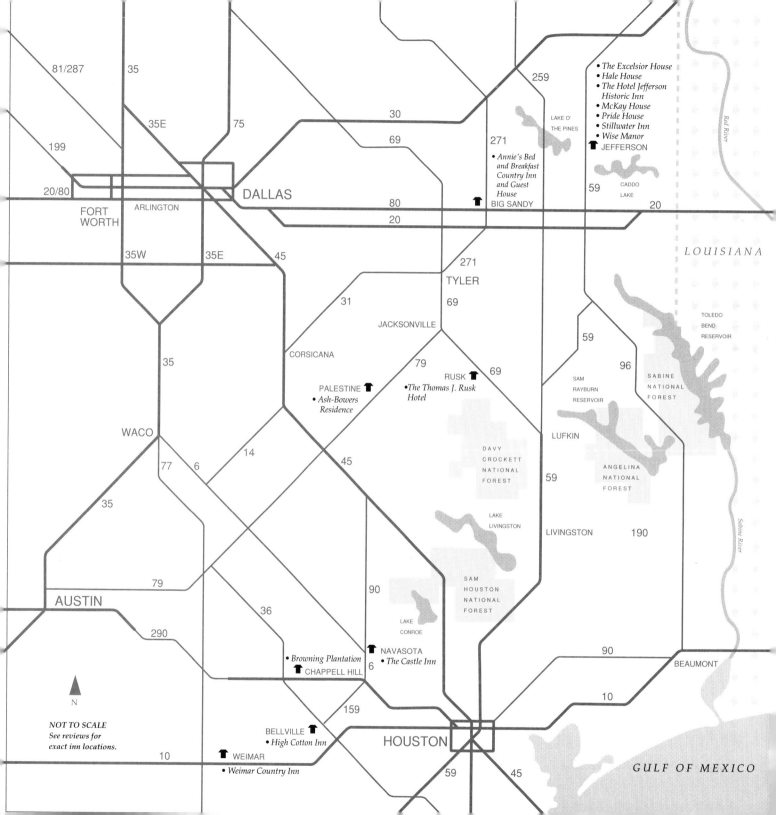

81/287

35

199

35E

75

20/80

DALLAS

FORT
WORTH

ARLINGTON

35W

35E

45

35

77   6

14

WACO

35

79

AUSTIN

290

N

NOT TO SCALE
*See reviews for
exact inn locations.*

10

36

BELLVILLE
• *High Cotton Inn*

WEIMAR
• *Weimar Country Inn*

30

69

259

• *The Excelsior House*
• *Hale House*
• *The Hotel Jefferson
  Historic Inn*
• *McKay House*
• *Pride House*
• *Stillwater Inn*
• *Wise Manor*

271

JEFFERSON

LAKE O'
THE PINES

Red River

• *Annie's Bed
and Breakfast
Country Inn
and Guest
House*

BIG SANDY

59

CADDO
LAKE

80

20

LOUISIANA

20

271

TYLER

69

JACKSONVILLE

31

CORSICANA

79

PALESTINE
• *Ash-Bowers
Residence*

RUSK
• *The Thomas J. Rusk
Hotel*

69

59

TOLEDO
BEND
RESERVOIR

96

SABINE
NATIONAL
FOREST

SAM
RAYBURN
RESERVOIR

LUFKIN

ANGELINA
NATIONAL
FOREST

59

DAVY
CROCKETT
NATIONAL
FOREST

45

LAKE
LIVINGSTON

LIVINGSTON

190

Sabine River

90

SAM
HOUSTON
NATIONAL
FOREST

LAKE
CONROE

• *Browning Plantation*
CHAPPELL HILL

NAVASOTA
• *The Castle Inn*

6

90

BEAUMONT

159

HOUSTON

10

59

45

GULF OF MEXICO

EAST TEXAS

Bordered roughly by Louisiana and Arkansas on the east, Oklahoma on the north, Dallas/Fort Worth on the west, and Houston on the south, East Texas is one of the most beautiful parts of the state. Here the Indians left their mark in ancient mounds. The Spanish arrived by the early sixteenth century, and for a few years in the seventeenth century, the French ruled this part of Texas. They were quickly routed again by the Spanish, who retained dominion over the area until 1821.

El Camino Real, the King's Highway, linked Mexico City with outposts in East Texas and Louisiana. Many of the state's most famous citizens, including Sam Houston and Stephen Austin, entered by this route. Visitors can still travel the King's Highway, which is now more or less paralleled by Highway 21 from San Antonio northeast to Louisiana.

East Texas flourished in the 1800s. Settlers became rich as their fields turned white with cotton. The crop was shipped east on riverboats that plied the many rivers and made wealthy cities of ports like Jefferson and Galveston. Magnificent antebellum homes, built by cotton kings and often still inhabited, dot the countryside.

Much of East Texas is still rural, punctuated by small towns with a charm that has not been wiped out by progress. Gothic town halls still dominate the central squares, and the tree-shaded streets are lined with homes built when craftsmanship was an art to be cherished. Steamboat Gothic, Eastlake Victorian, Queen Anne, and Greek Revival styles of architecture are the norm here, rather than the exception.

Nature, however, is by far East Texas' best attraction. In the spring, the fields glow with the colors of dogwood, bluebonnets, Indian paintbrush, and azaleas. Many of the towns hold special festivals celebrating this annual rainbow of blooms. Piney Woods and Big Thicket are just two of the better-known forests where the roads become tunnels of gold, red, and orange in the fall.

Lakes are almost as abundant as the trees, and fishing is among the best in the state. Many of the larger lakes offer sightseeing and dinner cruises on riverboats; boat tours of some of the mysterious bayous, such as Caddo Lake near Jefferson, are also available.

Getting There: The two major airports nearest East Texas are Dallas/Fort Worth and Houston.

Ladies in long, crisp, black-and-white Victorian dresses serve tea in the afternoon. Guests stay in rooms with names like Queen Victoria, Hideaway, and Garden View. If the quilt on the bed strikes your fancy, you can buy the pattern across the street at Annie's Attic.

Annie is Anita Gentry, whose mail-order needlecraft business has grown into a complex of enterprises. Each is housed in its own Victorian mansion amid gardens, fish ponds, and fountains, just off the highway that goes through the small East Texas town of Big Sandy.

Each of the three main buildings has a special history. The big blue house, which is now Annie's Tea Room, was built in 1925 by J. B. Rowe for his wife, Helen. During the 1920s and 30s the place served as a boardinghouse for local teachers, as did the yellow house that is now Annie's Attic.

The gray house, once known as the Tohill House and now the bed-and-breakfast inn, is the oldest of the three and also the most altered. Tohill, who bought the house in 1927, was the town's postmaster and mayor, and fourth owner of the single-story house built in 1901. That original building (measuring twenty by fifty feet) is now the parlor and dining room. Over the years the house was enlarged, but it was Annie who did the most reconstruction on what is now a three-story gingerbread delight with seven gables, thirteen guest rooms, and a variety of porches trimmed with white railings—all surrounded by gardens.

The inside of the inn is decorated with antiques, imported carpets, and handmade quilts (mostly from Annie's patterns). The lobby is filled with reproduction Victorian furniture in hues of soft rose and green. The large dining-room table is used for the games kept at the inn, and a VCR is available in the parlor.

The two rooms on the ground floor, Queen Victoria and Prince Albert, have outside entrances with wheelchair access, queen-size beds, hardwood floors, and Oriental carpets. Victoria is decorated in rose with a half-canopy over the brass bed and a fireplace. Albert is done in blues with a crocheted coverlet on the bed. Queen Anne is an attic suite with a queen-size bed, a private balcony, an antique tub, and a loft (reached by a spiral staircase) that contains twin beds covered with hand-crocheted spreads.

The Garret Room has a balcony and a sitting area. The Aviary Room has a sitting room with a sofa bed and a loft with a full-size bed. This room shares a corner of the house with the Twins' Corner, where the brass twin beds are covered in a fanciful child's quilt. Hideaway is done in lavenders, and Garden View looks over the gardens and fish pond across the street. The Loft, another of the balcony rooms, is done in pinks and lavenders with a brass-and-iron bed. The Sewing Room uses an

ANNIE'S BED AND BREAKFAST COUNTRY INN AND GUEST HOUSE

Highway 155 North, Box 928, Big Sandy, Texas 75755

Telephone: (214) 636-4355

Accommodations: thirteen rooms with twin, double, or queen-size beds; private and shared baths with tub, shower, or tub/shower; telephones in rooms; television with VCR in parlor.

Rates: inexpensive to expensive, full breakfast included (Continental on Saturday morning). Restaurant open for breakfast, lunch, and afternoon tea; dinner by reservation only, Sunday through Thursday. Children welcome. No pets.

Cards: AE, MC, V

No smoking inside the inn. Limited wheelchair access. Open all year.

old trundle machine as a table. The baths, both private and shared, have ornate brass and porcelain fixtures; some have antique tubs.

Room rates on weeknights include breakfast at Annie's Tea Room. Guests have three choices: Southern-style with biscuits and gravy, beef sausage, grits, and eggs; gourmet-style with a special entrée accompanied with fresh fruit and juice; or Continental-style with strawberry soup and homemade rolls.

The Weekend in the Country special offers a reduced-rate package for Friday and Saturday nights. This includes a Sunday breakfast in Annie's Tea Room and Continental breakfast in your room on Saturday: pecan rolls, cheese, crackers, and juice are kept in a small refrigerator fashioned like an antique safe. (A gourmet picnic brunch may be requested in advance for Saturday morning for an additional fee.) The refrigerators are also stocked with soft drinks and mineral water, which guests pay for on an honor system.

Annie's Tea Room is decorated in pink, rose, and white, with lace curtains and tablecloths and oak furniture. Upstairs is a gift shop, and in the garden out back is Annie's Pantry, where you can buy gourmet coffee and homemade candies.

Events are scheduled throughout the year at the inn, such as murder-mystery weekends, lawn art shows, a pecan festival in the fall, and a photo safari at the nearby private game ranch.

Getting There: Big Sandy is about two hours east of Dallas on Highway 80. When you reach Big Sandy, turn left onto Highway 155 north. Inn is a gray Victorian on the right.

RUSK/PALESTINE

This forested part of Texas was Indian territory back before recorded history, as evidenced by the Caddoan Mound State Park just a few miles south of Rusk. The park contains two ancient Indian ceremonial mounds as well as a reconstructed Caddoan house, a visitors' center, and an interpretive trail to guide curious wanderers.

Large numbers of white settlers came west only after the Cherokees had been driven into Oklahoma. By the 1800s, the towns of Rusk and Palestine had been founded and industry soon followed. The nearby town of New Birmingham, now a ghost town, became the headquarters for an early iron industry. To ship the ore, a railroad was built in the 1890s between Rusk and Palestine. Now known as the Texas State Railroad, it winds through woodlands and crosses twenty-six bridges, hauling tourists with the antique steam engines used in the movie *How the West Was Won* and the television series *Petticoat Junction.*

Rusk is the birthplace of Jim Hogg, the first native-born governor of the state of Texas; there is a replica of his mountain home at the Jim Hogg State Park. A walking tour of Rusk includes the nation's longest footbridge, which stretches 546 feet across a valley that was notorious for becoming a mire during the rainy season. Just north of town is Confederate Hill, where the town's young men sharpened their bayonets during the Civil War.

Palestine, situated between the Neches and Trinity rivers, has an authentic restoration of an 1833 church open for visitors, and the John H. Reagan Memorial Center offers exhibits that recount the town's pioneer past. Just outside town is the Scientific Balloon Base operated by NASA; launching schedules are available from the Chamber of Commerce.

This part of Texas is dotted with lakes and rivers. There is good fishing in well-stocked, spring-fed lakes, and picnic areas and hiking trails abound. Each year the dogwood blossoms herald spring.

Getting There: Rusk and Palestine are about 100 miles southeast of Dallas via Interstate 45 south to Highway 287 east.

When Henry Ash built his home in 1878, it was the most beautiful house in Palestine, according to an old newspaper article. The three-story building with Italianate details was also the only house in town that had a cupola. A. L. Bowers later purchased the house, adding the gingerbread trim and the three stained-glass windows over the staircase.

Bowers was superintendent of buildings and bridges for the International and Great Northern Railroad and president of Palestine Salt and Coal Company, as well as president or board member of several banks and companies throughout Texas. He also served as mayor of Palestine for a total of twenty years.

In about 1906 he added the European shower—then, as now, the talk of the town. A tower of circular pipes extended to the ceiling, and pinpoint holes in each horizontally-mounted circle emitted sprays of hot and cold water. Unfortunately the shower no longer works, but the adjacent hundred-gallon tub does.

After Bowers' death his son Andrew lived in the house, suffering from arthritis and an addiction to prescription drugs and alcohol. Piece by piece, he sold off the acreage around the house to support his habit, until only the present acre remained. After his death the house lay empty and vandals took everything of value.

ASH-BOWERS RESIDENCE

301 South Magnolia,
Palestine, Texas 75801

Telephone: (214) 729-1935

Accommodations: four rooms with twin, double, or queen-size beds; shared baths with tub or shower; telephone in hall; television in parlor.

Rates: moderate, full breakfast included. Children welcome. No pets.

No credit cards.

Texas Medallion. Open all year.

Ash-Bowers Residence

It changed ownership several times before James Jarrett and his wife bought the place in the early 1970s. Their extensive restoration was still underway in 1985 when they opened the house as a bed-and-breakfast inn. As Jim tells it, he's putting on "the old girl's fancy dress," repainting the house in white with blue and gold trim to bring out the colors in the stained glass.

The interior features both an "entertaining" parlor and a "sitting" parlor containing identical ebonized fireplaces with massive ceiling-high mirrors. Walk-through windows lead to the porch, and delicate Eastlake carvings grace the doorways of the downstairs rooms with their pocket sliding doors still in place. In the front parlor the heavy damask draperies hang from poles, just as they did when installed in 1897.

When the Jarretts bought the house, they found quite a bit of the Bowers' furniture stacked in the barn and bought the lot, including a sideboard and hand-carved walnut table and chairs that are now in the dining room. Old Andrew's chair is in the parlor where he liked to sit and read. The Knabe square grand piano came with the house, as did the cupid lamp on the bannister and the Tiffany glass in the ceiling fans.

Still standing on the grounds are the original carriage house, greenhouse, smokehouse, and servants' quarters, making the property one of the last complete Victorian homesteads in East Texas—and justly deserving of its Texas Medallion. On the north lawn is a gazebo with its original cistern and hand pump.

Jim, a makeup artist trained at Warner Brothers Studios, has turned the barn into a beauty parlor, but you can still see behind the original doors to where the carriage and six horses were stabled. The greenhouse is now the henhouse, where the Jarretts raise Aracuna hens from Brazil. These lay the colored "Easter" eggs that are served at the family-style breakfast along with scratch biscuits and homemade pear preserves, berry jam, or wild plum jelly. The Jarretts will also bring a tray of coffee or tea to your room before breakfast.

Rooms are large, with eleven-foot ceilings. At each end of the long hallway on the second floor is a shared bath, one with the famous European shower and oversized tub. The guest rooms, also off the hall, have carpets woven in an Axminster pattern. One room has ornate gingerbread trim in front of the bay windows where the iron bed stands. A second room has twin beds, and a third with a back staircase to the kitchen has a tailored look.

The house is located two blocks from downtown Palestine. This is a small, tree-shaded town, with parks sprinkled among the Victorian homes, many of which are being restored. The town lies at one end of the Palestine-Rusk State Park, and the Texas State Railroad train departs from the depot twice a day. The Dogwood Trails are held in the spring and the Fall Foliage Fair in October, and there is a home tour twice a year.

Getting There: From Dallas take Interstate 45 south to Corsicana and continue on Highway 287 east into Palestine. Turn left onto Palestine Avenue. At Sycamore, turn right to West Gooch. Turn right again to Magnolia; the Ash-Bowers Residence is on the corner of Gooch and Magnolia.

Thomas J. Rusk was one of the first United States senators from Texas. He was also a signer of the Texas Declaration of Independence, Secretary of War for the Republic of Texas, chief justice of the Texas Supreme Court, and a friend of Sam Houston.

The hotel that now bears his name blends a little Texas history with modern amenities. Renovated in 1979 and given a 1920's look, it is situated on the town square. The brick building sports an arched green awning that leads into a pleasant lobby with sandy pink walls, wing chairs, and Oriental carpets, all reproductions. The only original piece in the hotel is the front desk.

The coffee shop off the lobby is Art Deco in style, with custom-made chairs and soft track lighting. Here, the fare is traditional East Texas cooking, with entrées like pot roast and catfish. The Sam Houston Club, occupying the town's former bus station behind the hotel, is a private club; hotel guests are automatically members. Besides its bar, the club offers a more upscale version of East Texas cuisine.

Sunday through Friday the hotel offers a nominally priced noon buffet with soup and salad, two meats, two vegetables, dessert, and coffee. Room service is not available, but the hotel does have two restaurants. There are accommodations for banquets and small conventions in the Stephen F. Austin Room, and for parties of ten or less in the Governor's Room.

Unlike most small inns, all thirty-six rooms here are decorated alike, with brass beds and chenille spreads, reproduction dressers, wing chairs, period print wallpaper, and ceiling fans. The modern amenities include private baths, telephones, and televisions in the rooms. Some of the rooms are quite small (due to the addition of closets and private baths), but others, especially the suites, are spacious. Several of the baths are up a step from floor level to accommodate plumbing that was added to the old building. The favored rooms are those in the front overlooking the town square; the corner rooms with windows on both sides are bright and

THE THOMAS J. RUSK HOTEL
105 East Sixth Street,
Rusk, Texas 75785

Telephone: (214) 683-2556
or (800) 634-6513

Accommodations: thirty-six rooms with twin or double beds, one queen-size bed; private baths with tub/shower; telephones; television.

Rates: inexpensive to moderate, no meals included. Children welcome. Pets discouraged.

Cards: AE, MC, V

Meeting facilities. Open all year.

cheery. The suites are made up of either two rooms with two beds and a sitting room, or three rooms with one double and one twin bed.

Now famous as one end of the Texas State Railroad line, Rusk was originally farming country with a large tomato industry that lasted from the 1920s to World War II. After the war, the railroad went into decline and was not revived again until the early 1980s, when it became a tourist attraction. The area is deep in the Piney Woods of East Texas and the landscape is dotted with Southern pine, pecan, cedar, elm, and oak. In the spring, tourists come to see the Dogwood Trails.

Rusk is now a getaway for Houston and Dallas city folk who enjoy the quiet of the countryside and the fishing, boating, and waterskiing on nearby lakes. A self-guided walking tour of the quaint town is available, and the hotel staff leaves a package of information about the area in each room. They also have a shuttle to take guests to the train station.

During deer-hunting season, the hotel provides a hunter's package that includes, for a daily rate, a deer lease, transportation, Continental breakfast, sack lunch, and guide. The hotel will even arrange for the meat to be dressed by a local packer if you like.

Getting There: Rusk is an hour and a half from Dallas. From Palestine, take Highway 84 into Rusk. The hotel is on the town square on the left side of the street. Transportation available from municipal airport.

JEFFERSON

From New Orleans, the riverboats came up the Mississippi to the Red River, through Caddo Lake, and then up Cypress Bayou to Jefferson. The stern-wheelers hauled cotton, coal, iron ore, and munitions eastward, and settlers westward.

Founded in 1836, Jefferson became the "Gateway to Texas." The first riverboat arrived in 1844, captained by William Perry, who later built the Excelsior Hotel here; over two hundred steamboats a year followed, entering what is still called the Turning Basin. Jefferson grew and prospered, becoming the fifth-largest city in the state, and second only to Galveston as a port.

During the Civil War, Jefferson was an important supplier to the Confederacy, shipping hides, meat, and other foods. After the war, families headed west and many remained in the growing community, building elegant mansions. These remnants of antebellum aristocracy traveled in style on the well-appointed stern-wheelers and attended balls in first-class hotels like the Excelsior.

So heady with their success were Jeffersonians that when railway magnate Jay Gould asked them to give him land for a railroad right-of-way, they demanded that he buy it. Gould refused, predicted the end of Jefferson, and took his railroad to Marshall, just a few miles away.

The railroad was completed in 1873, and it did diminish Jefferson's importance as a port. Then, later that year, the final blow came. The Army Corps of Engineers used nitroglycerin charges to permanently remove a log jam on the Red River, which eventually lowered the level of Caddo Lake and Big Cypress Bayou. The water was no longer deep enough for the Mississippi riverboats, and Jefferson's days as a port were over.

Jefferson made the headlines again when it was the scene of a sensational murder trial that dragged on for years. On January 31, 1877, Bessie Moore, a flamboyant young woman whose jewel collection gave her the nickname "Diamond Bessie," crossed the footbridge over Big Cypress with her companion Abe Rothschild. Several days later, her body was found on the banks of the bayou. Rothschild was brought to trial and eventually acquitted. The murder was listed as "unsolved." Diamond Bessie was buried in the local cemetery; adding to the mystery was the unexplained appearance, in the 1930s, of a headstone that still marks her grave.

Over one hundred acres of this small East Texas town are listed on the National Register as a historic district; self-guided tours are available from the Chamber of Commerce. The Atalanta, the private railroad car that belonged to Jay Gould and his actress wife, is on display across the street from the Excelsior Hotel, and tours may be arranged at the hotel desk daily from nine to five.

Riverboat cruises on Big Cypress Bayou, offered mid-March through late October, give visitors a glimpse of abandoned mills and factories that once lined this busy steamboat passage. Several homes are open daily for tours, including the House of the Seasons, named for its stained-glass windows representing seasons of the year. Other homes are open only during Pilgrimage. This annual event, held the first weekend in May, was started by the Jessie Allen Wise Garden Club in the early 1940s. A similar Christmas Candlelight Tour is held the first weekend in December. During Pilgrimage, the local theater group re-enacts "The Diamond Bessie Murder Trial," and during the Candlelight Tour there is a Victorian Christmas play.

An antique doll collection is displayed on the first floor of the Carnegie Library. And no stay in Jefferson is complete without a visit to the exhibits at the Jefferson Historical Museum, a surrey ride through the brick streets, and a look at the twenty-eight (at last count) antiques shops.

Getting There: Jefferson is three hours east of Dallas. Take Interstate 20 east to Marshall, then Highway 59 north to Jefferson.

In 1882 Jay Gould scrawled "End of Jefferson, Texas" in the Excelsior House guest register when the citizens of Jefferson refused to give him a right-of-way for his railroad. During Jefferson's heyday as a bustling river port, the register read like a *Who's Who*: Ulysses S. Grant, Rutherford B. Hayes, Oscar Wilde, John Jacob Astor, W. H. Vanderbilt, and, of course, Jay Gould. Today some of these registers, dating back to 1877, lie open in a display cabinet in the lobby of the Excelsior.

The hotel, originally known as the Irving House, was built by Captain William Perry in the 1850s. Perry operated a dredge boat that kept Big Cypress Bayou open for the steamboats. During the Civil War, the hotel was a gathering place for Confederate soldiers, and about this time the first addition was built. After Perry's death the hotel changed hands and names several times before Kate Wood purchased it in 1877. When steamboats could no longer come as far as Jefferson, it looked as if Gould's prediction that "grass will grow in your streets, and bats will roost in your belfries" might come true. But the town held on, and so did the hotel.

Jefferson's revitalization as a tourist mecca began in the early 1960s. The Excelsior House was for sale, and a group of enterprising women known as the Jessie Allen Wise Garden Club purchased the hotel, signing their husbands' names in order to secure the bank loan. The garden club formed the Jefferson Historical Restoration and Preservation Corporation and began restoring the hotel, with a great deal of support from the townsfolk and help from the local craftsmen, who donated their skills. Each original piece of furniture was refinished, and the collection was augmented with other antique pieces, some donated, some purchased.

The garden club still owns the hotel, and its members run the place with the style and graciousness of an old Southern home. All rooms are decorated with antiques of cherry, maple, mahogany, and rosewood, and many of the floors are covered with Oriental carpets. The historic rooms are spectacular—so spectacular that check-in occurs only after the two afternoon tours are over. For guests the tour is free, for others there is a nominal charge.

The Presidential Suite is made up of two rooms and the original bath that was once shared by the entire wing of the hotel. The Hayes Room, where Rutherford B. Hayes once stayed, has a ten-foot tester bed, red walls, and the original chandelier. The Grant Room, done in gold and mahogany, has a portrait of Grant, traded about seventy-five years ago for a night's stay at the hotel.

The Rosewood Room is also called the Lady Bird Room after Mrs. Johnson, a frequent visitor. Carved rosewood distinguishes two Napoleon beds and a petticoat table (a small table with a mirror underneath so ladies can see if their petticoats

THE EXCELSIOR HOUSE

211 West Austin Street,
Jefferson, Texas 75657

Telephone: (214) 665-2513

Accommodations: fourteen rooms with twin or double beds; private baths with tub, shower, or tub/shower; telephones in hall; television in rooms.

Rates: inexpensive to moderate, plantation breakfast extra and by reservation only. Children welcome. No pets.

No credit cards.

Limited wheelchair access. Texas Medallion, National Register. Closed Christmas Eve and the week of Spring Pilgrimage.

are showing). And, of course, there is a Jay Gould Room. The high, ornately carved bed is of Circassian walnut from Russia, and there is, appropriately enough, a replica of a railroad desk in the room.

The Excelsior's ballroom was the backdrop for many nineteenth-century social functions, such as the Queen Mab festivities, Jefferson's version of Mardi Gras. The hardwood floor is covered with an Oriental carpet, and a crystal chandelier hangs from the pressed-tin ceiling. The Belter table was carved from a single piece of rosewood, and the square grand piano was reportedly brought to Jefferson by Captain Perry on his riverboat.

Breakfast is served in the dining room beyond the columns at the end of the ballroom. It is the only meal the hotel provides, and even guests must make reservations. The plantation breakfast consists of ham, grits, eggs, and orange-blossom muffins. You may dine either on the sun porch that overlooks the courtyard and fountain or in the formal dining room with its mahogany Chippendale table and French chandelier of gilt-and-blue Sevres porcelain.

Also owned by the garden club is Jay Gould's private railroad car, which, with a bit of poetic justice, had been abandoned on a siding. The club purchased the Atalanta, and it now sits across the street from the hotel. Anyone wishing to tour the car may ask the desk clerk at the Excelsior between nine and five daily.

Getting There: Take Broadway to the "V" and bear right onto Polk. Go six blocks to Austin and turn right; the Excelsior House is on the right.

In 1851 the Hotel Jefferson was used to store cotton bales for shipment on the riverboats that waited in the Turning Basin just outside the front door. Then, in 1873, the log jam was destroyed, the river level fell, and Jefferson lost its link with the Mississippi. The shipping town's era as the "Gateway to Texas" was over.

The Turning Basin was eventually filled in, and the hotel's front entrance is now on Austin Street right in the middle of Jefferson's historic district—just a block from the museum and next door to Jay Gould's railroad car.

Over the years the building served as the Crystal Palace International Bar Room, Grigsby Hotel, The Orton Building, Pruitt House, and the New Jefferson Hotel. From 1882 until the 1930s the hotel was run, in succession, by three indomitable women: Mrs. Grigsby, Mrs. Thompson, and Mrs. Schluter. Major restoration was done in the late 1970s, when private baths were installed.

Unlike many of the buildings in town, The Hotel Jefferson is an unadorned, square brown structure with an overhang that extends over the sidewalk on two

THE HOTEL JEFFERSON HISTORIC INN

124 Austin Street,
Jefferson, Texas 75657

Telephone: (214) 665-2631

Accommodations: twenty-four rooms with double, queen-, or king-size beds; private baths with tub or shower; no telephones; black-and-white television.

Rates: inexpensive, no meals included. Children welcome. No pets.

Cards: MC, V

Limited wheelchair access. Convention facilities. Open all year.

sides. The guest rooms, mostly on the second floor, are quite large and range in style from an early-American country look to formal Victorian.

The king- and queen-size beds are reproductions, but most of the other furniture is antique. One room has a sleigh bed and one of twelve original claw-foot tubs. The Delk Suite, named for the owners who did the restoration in the 1970s, has a carved wooden bed set up on a dias and draped in organdy. Another suite has two reproduction white-iron and brass beds and ornate cupid-adorned lamps.

The lobby is filled with antique velvet sofas and chairs, marble-topped tables, and a hotel desk from the 1920s. On display under a glass case is an old guest register found beneath the stairs during renovation. The front desk holds other papers from years past: menus, grocery lists, and employee records. The staff encourages guests to use the sitting areas and to get to know one another, so there is always a pot of coffee brewing. No meals are served at the hotel, but the former dining room has been leased out as the Catfish Inn, which serves lunch and dinner Wednesday through Sunday.

Getting There: Take Broadway to the "V" and bear right on Polk. Go six blocks to Austin and turn right; the hotel is on the left.

The big yellow house with white trim and a wraparound porch, now called Pride House, looked like a haunted house from an old Hitchcock movie when Sandy and Ray Spaulding bought it. Both front and back porches had collapsed, and one room was stacked with pieces of gingerbread trim that had fallen off the structure. But it was solid and built to last, not to mention romantic, with stained-glass windows in every room.

A lumberyard owner named Mr. Brown constructed the house toward the end of the last century. According to Mr. Brown's son (who came to see the old house after it had opened as a bed-and-breakfast inn), whenever an exceptionally fine piece of pine or cypress came through the lumberyard, the foreman sent it up to the lot for Mr. Brown's house.

This is the sixth old house the Spauldings have restored. It is named for their son, Pride, and run by Sandy's mother, Ruthmary Jordan. After tourists discovered Jefferson, The Excelsior House was turning away guests on the weekends. Ruthmary opened the four upstairs rooms in the mid-1970s to handle the overflow. So far, no one has disputed her claim that Pride House is the oldest B&B in Texas.

Family pieces are scattered throughout the house, but to avoid a museumlike atmosphere the old has been mixed with the new. The Green Room has emerald-

PRIDE HOUSE

409 East Broadway,
Jefferson, Texas 75657

Telephone: (214) 665-2675

Accommodations: ten rooms with double, queen-, or king-size beds, some with fireplaces; private baths with tub, shower, or tub/shower; telephones and television on request.

Rates: moderate, fancy Continental breakfast included. Children over ten welcome. No pets.

Cards: MC, V

Texas Medallion. Open all year.

Pride House

green walls, antique white wicker furniture, and a white-iron and brass bed. Ruthmary lays a fire on the hearth here on chilly nights. The Blue Room has four stained-glass windows and contains antique white French furniture that belonged to Ruth Mary's husband's parents. But the king-size bed is modern, and a wallcovering of blue-and-white-striped mattress ticking serves as a headboard, with a gold clock in the center.

Ruthmary calls the Bay Room her "lusty Victorian." The brass headboard on the king-size bed is actually the head and foot of an antique bed welded together and hung on the wall. The rest of the furniture is Eastlake Victorian, and the ceiling is painted dark blue with gold stars. The West Room is done in Victorian red with a white-iron double bed, stained-glass windows, and a claw-foot tub in the bathroom. You'll find bubble bath and bath salts, too, as in all the rooms.

Downstairs is the romantic Golden Era with its half-tester bed draped in lace and set in a bay with a stained-glass window. The Carrie Pool has more of a country flair, with a primitive iron double bed.

Each room also contains a book that guests are asked to sign and write comments in. The upstairs hall has a small library of paperbacks; you're invited to take one to read or leave one you've already finished. Guests gather downstairs in the parlor, which is delightfully cluttered with plants and knickknacks in the Victorian manner; here too is a working fireplace.

Behind the house is the Dependency, built in 1888 as servants' quarters. Moved from another part of the property, it has four additional rooms, named for family and friends and done in more of a country style as befits its origins.

Pride's Room is a child's attic room set under the eaves, with the bed under the slanted roof and the ceiling papered and edged with eyelet to represent a canopy. It has a small desk filled with books and magazines, a basket of seashells, children's drawings on the walls, and pegs to hang your clothes on. The claw-foot tub is behind a screen, and the longhorns for hanging towels were Pride's idea.

Katie's Room, across the tiny landing, is entered through a private balcony. Carol's Room, on the first floor, has a tiny front porch with a swing. The suite, done in gingham blue, is the largest room in the Dependency, with a living/sitting area and a wood-burning stove.

Coffee is served early in the morning in the upstairs hall of the main house and in the kitchen of the Dependency. Later, Ruthmary sets out a breakfast that might include fresh croissants, poached pears, and sausage, which guests take to their rooms on silver trays.

Getting There: Pride House is four blocks from the intersection of Highway 59 and Broadway, on the left.

Hale House is a small, green-gabled building. An arched gate at the side of the house leads to lovely gardens, and an ornate wrought-iron bench graces the front porch. Off the entry hall is a parlor filled with turn-of-the-century antiques of oak and pine. Lace curtains cover the etched windows, and the wallpaper replicates the pattern used in Ford's Theater circa 1865. Here, too, is a picture of May Belle Hale, who was born in the house and lived there until her death in 1968.

A spinster, May Belle taught music at the school that once stood across the street, the only school in the county. Some children lived too far away to commute on a daily basis, so May Belle took them in as boarders. She was also instrumental in raising the challenge money for the Jefferson Museum, and there is a room in the public library dedicated to her. May Belle's morning room is now used as an office by the present owners, Linda and Mark Leonard, who bought the old house in 1984.

The six large guest rooms, all on the second floor, are filled with plants and decorated in muted tones of peach, rose, and blue, with turn-of-the-century furnishings of iron, mahogany, pine, oak, and wicker. The queen-size beds are, of course, modern, and Linda has hung paintings above the beds instead of using headboards. Country touches include Laura Ashley comforters, quilts, or crocheted spreads, wallpaper in a tiny Victorian print, braided rugs on the hardwood floors, and rocking chairs. Not all rooms have private baths, but the shared bath has a large claw-foot tub. The rooms at the back overlook the gardens; those in front overlook the park.

If the birds singing in the garden waken a guest early, there's always coffee in the upstairs hall by 6:30 a.m. A full breakfast is served later on the long, polished table in the dining room or on wicker furniture on the sun porch that overlooks the gardens. Coffee is made Louisiana-style with chicory, and breakfast is "gourmet Southern," with selections such as Spanish omelets, sausage quiche, yeast pastries, and muffins made with hand-picked blueberries. Linda's specialty is cheese grits, the only recipe she refuses to share. Hanging against the dark blue walls in the dining room is a pink-and-white quilt, dated 22 March 1839, which was hand stitched by one of Linda's ancestors. Guests are asked to make themselves at home and often gather in the spacious parlor, play cards on the sun porch, or borrow the tandem bicycle for a tour of the historic district just a few blocks away.

Getting There: From Broadway, turn right on Alley. Go two blocks to Walker, turn right, continue to Line and turn right again. Continue on Line for three blocks; Hale House is on the left.

HALE HOUSE BED AND BREAKFAST

702 South Line Street, Jefferson, Texas 75657

Telephone: (214) 665-8877

Accommodations: six rooms with double or queen-size beds; private and shared baths with tub or tub/shower; no telephones; no television.

Rates: moderate, full breakfast included. Children welcome. No pets.

Cards: MC, V

Smoking is not encouraged. Open all year.

McKay House

Owners Tom and Peggy Taylor want guests to have more than just a good night's rest—they want them to have an experience. That's why a guest at the McKay House can crawl into bed wearing a Victorian lady's dressing gown or a man's sleep shirt, snuggle under handmade quilts, and bathe with Crabtree & Evelyn toiletries that exude the fragrances of a bygone era. Guests are greeted with homemade tea cakes and lemonade when they arrive, and in the morning Peggy dresses in period costume to serve breakfast.

The setting for this Victorian experience was built in 1851 by Daniel N. Alley, one of the cofounders of Jefferson, though today the house bears the name of its third owner, Hecktor McKay—one of the defense attorneys for Abe Rothschild in the celebrated Diamond Bessie murder trial. The single-story, Colonial-style house has a neat, tailored appearance, with four columns supporting the wide front porch, blue shutters alongside the tall windows, and a white picket fence.

When the Taylors bought the house in 1984, it was a disaster. The interior walls were unpainted, unpapered sheetrock, and old carpet covered the heart-of-pine floors. It took nine months of hard work to put the house to rights, but it was worth the effort. The McKay House is now booked a year in advance for the Pilgrimage and the Candlelight Tour, and the guest list includes Lady Bird Johnson and Alex Haley.

The four rooms in the main house open off the long, wide hall at the center of the original building. Lace curtains, Schumacher wallpapers, and antiques collected by the Taylors embellish the rooms. Imported chocolate candy, with a love note inside, is set out in each room when guests arrive, as is a vase of fresh flowers. (When the fresh flowers dry up, they become the potpourri found throughout the inn.) The quilts in the rooms were all handmade especially for the inn.

The McKay Room, done in blues and burgundy, has a gas fireplace, a bookcase filled with reading material, a rocker to relax in, and a private bath with a claw-foot tub. The red-and-lavender-hued Quilt Room has quilts on the wall as well as the bed; the private bath has a marble sink and a beveled three-way mirror. The Spinning Room takes its name from the working spinning wheel, carding basket, and winder in one corner. It is decorated with American Victorian furniture. The Jefferson Room is the smallest, with twin beds. Decorated in tones of blue and brown, its style is more Colonial to match the house. The small bath with a mirrored shower between the Spinning and Jefferson rooms can be shared, or guests can take both rooms as a suite with private bath.

Behind the main house is the Sunday house. This hundred-year-old dogtrot-style building has two more rooms with private baths and a shared parlor. The

McKAY HOUSE

306 East Delta Street, Jefferson, Texas 75657

Telephone: (214) 665-7322 or 348-1929

Accommodations: six rooms with twin or double beds, some with fireplaces; private and shared baths with tub, shower, or tub/shower; no telephones; no television.

Rates: moderate, full breakfast included. Children welcome in the Sunday house. No pets.

Cards: MC, V

No smoking inside the inn. Texas Medallion. Open all year.

Keeping Room is done in a primitive style, much as a one-room log cabin might have been, with an open stone hearth cluttered with kettles, and an old iron bedstead. The Sunday Room across the shared parlor is done in a lacy country style with a double rocker in front of the wood-burning fireplace, a high wooden headboard, and a Murphy bed for an extra person. Children are not encouraged in the main house, but are welcome in the Sunday house.

Many newlyweds stay at the McKay House, and if they prefer, Peggy will serve them breakfast in bed. Others eat in the morning room, which was added in the early 1970s, or on pleasant days in the brick patio. This "gentleman's" breakfast consists of cheese biscuits, honey-cured ham, strawberry bread, fresh fruit with orange sauce, and juice, tea, or coffee. The Taylors bought their 140-piece china breakfast set in an antiques shop, but there were no cups until they found a local woman who painted cups to match the china.

Getting There: From the stoplight, take Broadway to Alley. Turn right on Alley and go four blocks to Delta. Turn right; the inn is on the left.

T he exterior of the Stillwater Inn, like most of the buildings in Jefferson, is Victorian; it's an 1893 gray Eastlake trimmed in white and blue that sits on the main street. The inside, however, is totally unexpected. The inn's decor is restfully spare and clean. The parlor's oak floors were laid over the original pine during a major restoration in the 1930s. A high pine mantel is set against the far wall, and on chilly days there is a roaring fire. Clean, uncluttered lines are carried out in the simple, unvarnished furniture. Pine daybeds are upholstered in white, and an old bellows sits before the fire as a table. Dried-flower arrangements complement the setting.

Owner Bill Stewart, a former Dallas chef, opened the Stillwater Inn as a restaurant in 1983; its success has prompted other innkeepers in town to recommend it to guests looking for an excellent place to dine. The first floor is taken over by the restaurant, and tastefully decorated (as is the entire inn) by Bill's wife, Sharon.

Guests may sip a glass of wine in the parlor while waiting for dinner, or wander into the small bar area, which shares a see-through fireplace with the dining room. The bar itself is a massive ebonized oak piece, and one wall of the room is a floor-to-ceiling wine rack. The restaurant's cluster of small tables seats only sixty. The cuisine, which is mostly French and is prepared by Bill, includes such tempting entrées as grilled shrimp, smoked Cornish hen, grilled breast of duck, and a daily fresh fish special that might be salmon or red snapper.

STILLWATER INN

203 East Broadway,
Jefferson, Texas 75657

Telephone: (214) 665-8415

Accommodations: four rooms with twin or queen-size beds; private baths with tub and hand shower; telephones in common areas; color television in rooms.

Rates: moderate to expensive, full breakfast included. Restaurant open for lunch and dinner Wednesday through Sunday; club memberships available automatically for inn guests. Well-behaved children welcome. No pets; boarding kennel just around the corner.

Cards: MC, V

No smoking in rooms. Open all year.

The B&B, which wasn't opened until May of 1986, is on the second floor in what was once an 1,800-square-foot attic. Although there is access to the rooms from the restaurant, a private entrance leads directly to the back stairs.

Upstairs, the Stewarts chose to construct only three bedrooms with two large common areas for the guests' use. Here, dramatically pitched ceilings, skylights, and stained-glass windows give a feeling of openness. The furniture is more contemporary with a few antiques, brass candlesticks, and framed eyelet handkerchiefs sprinkled about. A Shaker settee and a wall of bookcases occupy the common areas; pine trim complements plain white walls touched with blue.

Most of the furniture upstairs has been handcrafted, like the four-poster beds that just fit under the eaves in two of the rooms. Another room has a bed with no headboard, a tile-topped dresser, and an armless settee, while the largest room has two beds, tucked away in separate nooks under the dormers for privacy. In all the bedrooms you'll find eyelet or lace curtains, quilts on the beds, and private baths with black slate floors, hand-held brass showers, and claw-foot tubs.

The small cottage at the back has a kitchenette and a small bath with shower only. The lofted ceiling is beamed, the room is furnished in pine and wicker, and there is a small front porch for sitting in the evening.

In the morning, the Stewarts bring a tray of freshly ground and brewed coffee for the early risers. A full breakfast is served downstairs in the dining room.

Getting There: From Highway 59, turn left on Broadway; the inn is one block down on the left.

Innkeeper Katherine Wise has lived in this house all her life, and it is filled with three generations of family possessions. In the dining room, under the crystal chandelier that hangs from an ornate plaster ceiling medallion, the table is set with silver, china, crystal, and a centerpiece of silk flowers. Against one wall is a glass breakfront displaying Katherine's parents' wedding presents. The family silver service sits on a tea cart, and the house is filled with pictures of her ancestors and paintings by her daughter.

Built in 1874, the small, peach-colored cottage with white gingerbread trim is nestled behind a white wrought-iron fence and surrounded by pecan trees as old as the building itself. Here Katherine, the town historian, entertains her guests and, in her spare time, does much of the research for home owners interested in applying for a Texas Medallion. She also does genealogical research, which takes her all over the United States and Europe. Her own genealogy is fascinating; Katherine's

WISE MANOR

312 Houston,
Jefferson, Texas 75657

Telephone: (214) 665-2386

Accommodations: three rooms with double or single beds; private and shared baths with tub and hand shower; telephones on request; television in parlor.

Rates: moderate, Continental breakfast included. Children welcome. No pets.

No credit cards.

Texas Medallion. Open all year.

grandmother-in-law was Jessie Allen Wise who, with the women of her garden club, did so much for Jefferson.

Wise Manor has three guest rooms. The cheerful first-floor room with the bright, rose-patterned paper has a four-poster spindle bed with a lace spread and lace curtains in the windows. The bath across the hall has an old-fashioned claw-foot tub. The two rooms on the second floor have a bath between them; they can be rented either together as a suite with a private bath or as separate rooms with a shared bath.

The larger room has a double and a single bed, both with quilts and tall, carved headboards. There is a stained-glass lamp on the marble-topped table. The smaller room has stenciled walls, and old chicken crates provide extra shelf space for blankets and pillows. On the bed are three stuffed bears that Katherine's mother made for her when she went off to college.

Katherine wants her guests to feel at home, to make coffee when they please and to relax in the cozy Victorian parlor with its velvet chairs, settees, and footstools. Here she serves wine in the afternoon. In the morning, coffee comes in handpainted mugs, and breakfast consists of fruit compote, ham-and-cheese croissants, and juice.

Getting There: From Broadway, turn right onto Alley. Go two blocks to Walker. Turn left, continue to Line and turn right. Just before Line Street dead ends, take left fork (Houston); the house is on the left.

This stately brick house sits far enough off the highway to be totally screened by foliage in the summer. Not even the white-trimmed hexagonal tower is visible from the street. The interior is elegant, with plaster ceiling medallions, floors inlaid with five different kinds of wood, and walls of curly pine and the now-extinct tiger oak. The house has eight bay windows, transoms and doors of beveled glass, and a twenty-foot stained-glass window over the staircase.

Ward Birrell Templeman built the house in 1893 as a wedding present for his bride, Annie. Templeman, with his father, was a cotton factor, as well as owner of an elite general store and part-owner of Schumacher Oil.

Tim and Helen Urquhart bought the house in 1983 and filled it with the results of their thirty-three years of antiques collecting. The parlor, with its ornately carved white fireplace, is done in rose with gilt touches and a pink porcelain chandelier; the colors are repeated in the Oriental carpet. Vintage dolls lounge on armless velvet chairs, originally designed for women in hoop skirts. The windows

THE CASTLE INN

1403 East Washington,
Navasota, Texas 77868

Telephone: (409) 825-8051

Accommodations: four rooms with double beds; private baths with tub or shower; no telephones; no television.

Rates: moderate, Continental breakfast included. Children over thirteen welcome. No pets.

Cards: MC, V

No smoking in rooms. Open all year.

The Castle Inn

are covered in lace; the family Bible sits in a corner. The dining room walls are peach, and in contrast, the library is done in blues.

Upstairs, a spot favored by guests is the open landing with a semicircular window seat in the hexagonal tower and walk-through windows opening to a porch. Here Helen lays out breakfast on trays: homemade bran muffins in bread warmers, fruit set out on ice, coffee and juice in insulated carafes—all ready for guests when they awaken.

In one room, a carved half-tester from Tennessee is set in a window bay. Another room has a carved walnut-burl bed from an estate in New York, with removable panels in the headboards and footboards to allow evening breezes to flow through in summer. Some beds are covered with handmade quilts, others with crocheted coverlets. Marble-topped dressers and tables are scattered about and windows are covered in lace. The bridal suite at the back of the house has a rosewood plantation bed tucked into a three-sided window bay overlooking the gardens.

Throughout the house are salesmen's furniture samples, which to the uninitiated eye look like doll furniture: a tiny dresser with marble top, a Morris chair, a brass bed, and a rocking chair, each occupied by a handmade doll.

In the afternoons, Helen and Tim serve cheese, fruit, and refreshments on the porch or in the parlor. With advance notice, they will prepare a festive dinner for a minimum of three to four couples. They have no liquor license, so guests are expected to bring their own dinner wine. The Urquharts also give group tours, which include lunch on the porch.

This was cotton country in the nineteenth century, and just a few miles from Navasota is Washington-on-the-Brazos, the first capital of the Republic of Texas. Navasota is also just nineteen miles from the site of the annual Renaissance Festival. The first weekend in May brings Nostalgia Days, when the townspeople dress in Victorian costume and set up exhibits of arts, crafts, dolls, and quilts. At Christmas there are candlelight tours of various homes in the town.

The Castle Inn sits on two acres of tree-shaded grounds with fish ponds, fountains, cast-iron tables and chairs, and even a tree swing. In the spring, bluebonnets blanket the countryside.

Getting There: From Houston take Highway 45 north to Conroe. Go east on Highway 105 to Navasota, north on Highway 6 for one mile, then back onto Highway 105. Turn left on Washington (the main street in town). Just before the grocery store is a dirt road; the inn is 300 feet down this road. Transportation available from municipal airport.

Once cotton country, this part of Texas is now used mostly for cattle, horses, and weekend retreats. The High Cotton Inn has become a getaway spot for Austin, San Antonio, and Houston residents who come to relax and escape the big-city tension. The gray-and-burgundy house, located not far from the center of town, has a two-story porch that wraps around a curved, window-filled bay.

The house was built around 1906 by Charles Frederick Hellmuth who, like most people in the area, was in cotton. A descendant of one of the earliest German settlers in Texas, he had a thousand acres of land, several general stores in various small towns, and his own mill to extract oil from cottonseed. To preserve family traditions and ensure that each new household was properly run, his five sons were expected to bring their new brides home for a year of "training" from Mrs. Hellmuth.

Today, Anna and George Horton own the inn. Guests are greeted by the rich tones of a grandfather clock. Over the wide doorways between the parlor and the dining room is a carved spindle fringe. The house is furnished with family heirlooms mingled with pieces picked up here and there. Against one wall is a Collard and Collard piano carved from rosewood. On the end tables between the settee and chairs is a pillbox collection. The pine floors are covered in Oriental carpets.

The five-foot-wide dining table would be bigger than the dining room if the Hortons decided to add all twelve leaves. Even so, there are evenings when they could use the space. Dinner at the inn, served Friday and Saturday for groups and by reservation only, is sumptuous. But guests staying in one of the five rooms upstairs are treated to an equally sumptuous plantation breakfast of eggs, sausage, grits, biscuits and cream gravy, a sweet bread such as rum cake, coffee, and fruit. If that isn't enough, the Hortons make cookies and candies that they sell at the inn and in various Texas cities.

The stairway's curved pine banister sweeps past a mirror that covers the wall on the top landing. A small sitting room on the second floor has access to the second-story porch. The five guest rooms upstairs are named for relatives and friends. The Sallie Sewall Room is named after George's grandmother, whose ball gown adorns the dressmaker's model in the upstairs sitting area. The room has a king-size brass bed and a clothes chest built by George's father. The Jay Bute Room, named for the friend who provided all the paint and paper for the renovation, has a high double bed and a mirrored armoire.

Uncle Buster's room—he also has a hall at Rice University named for him— has a carved bed and two of the many family portraits that hang throughout the house. Ella Campbell was George's aunt, and her room (which has a double and a twin bed) is decorated with pine wainscoting and green wallpaper. The Bobby

HIGH COTTON INN

214 South Live Oak,
Bellville, Texas 77418

Telephone: (409) 865-9796

Accommodations: five rooms with twin, double, queen-, or king-size beds; shared baths with tub or shower; telephones; television.

Rates: moderate, full breakfast included. Dinner Friday and Saturday for groups and by reservation only. Well-behaved children welcome. No pets.

No credit cards.

No smoking inside hotel. Open all year.

Russell room, named for another friend, is the most masculine of the rooms and overlooks the swimming pool in the back.

Special touches include embroidered pillowcases, lace curtains, and quilts. The five rooms share two baths, one with a claw-foot tub and one with a shower; guests take their pick. The Hortons can also arrange off-site boarding for the family pet.

The area is noted for its antiques shops, and nearby are Stephen F. Austin State Park, music festivals at Round Top, and the restored village of Henckle Square, just down the road. At Winedale is a folk-life research center.

Getting There: From Houston take Interstate 10 west. Take the second Sealy exit and head north on Highway 36 into Bellville. Go through town, around the town square, and continue on until you see the stoplight. Two blocks before the stoplight, turn right; the inn is on the right.

Chappell Hill is such a tiny town that you see no highway signs indicating it until you get there. The town itself is a quaint, restored little community tucked into the trees along the side of the highway. One of the best reasons for coming to Chappell Hill, however, is the inn on the other side of the highway. Guests drive down a long, tree-lined dirt road that suddenly opens onto a vista of the plantation standing majestically amid an expanse of grounds.

When Dick Ganchan, an executive with a Houston construction company, and his wife, Mildred, bought the property in 1980, elegant lawn parties and ladies in hoop skirts were hardly the vision conjured by the site. Already on the National Register of Historic Places, the building of weathered cypress (cut from trees grown on the property) had a gaping hole where the front door belonged. Windows were boarded up, and sunlight, coming through the third-story roof, streaked across cypress planks on the first floor.

During the restoration, the historical integrity of the house was maintained by utilizing attic space and chimneys for duct work. Closets were turned into half baths without altering the walls. After three years of hard labor on their Greek Revival mansion, the Ganchans graciously welcomed guests.

Colonel W. W. Browning was a leading citizen of Chappell Hill and his plantation, built in 1857, was the focus of the town's social life. Besides being a community leader in civic, religious, and agricultural affairs, he was a stockholder in the company that built the Washington County Railroad and was involved with one of the first documented efforts to produce oil in Texas. Since Browning was also the founder of Soule University and President of Chappell Hill Female College,

BROWNING PLANTATION

Route 1, Box 8,
Chappell Hill, Texas 77426

Telephone: (409) 836-6144
or (713) 626-9592

Accommodations: six rooms with double or queen-size beds; shared and private baths; telephones available in main house; no television.

Rates: expensive to very expensive, plantation breakfast included. Children over twelve welcome. No pets.

No credit cards.

No smoking inside inn. Texas Medallion, National Register. Open all year.

Browning Plantation

commencement exercises for students were often held at the house. Then the Civil War came. Browning not only invested heavily in the Confederacy, but his only son was killed in the fighting.

The layout of his six-thousand-square-foot house is simple. Each floor has four large, square rooms off the wide hallway, which has doors at each end to catch the summer breezes. The cypress-board walls have been painted in pastels as they would have been in Browning's day. The faux-bois grained paneling, for which the house was once noted, has been carefully repainted by one of the Ganchans' daughters.

Most of the furniture in the house was purchased by the Ganchans in England. Exceptions are the antiques in the parlor, which once belonged to a chief justice of the New York Supreme Court. An old Civil War map table and a square grand piano dominate the library, and the dining room has a pair of stained-glass doors.

Mildred serves breakfast at the English dining table, which seats eighteen. If there is a full house, she makes a plantation breakfast of sausage, cheese, and egg casserole served with fruit compote or fresh fruit, grits, hot biscuits, and homemade jellies and jams. If there are only one or two couples, she pares the meal down to scrambled eggs, sausage or bacon, grits, and biscuits. For special occasions Mildred prepares formal dinners, which are elegant and expensive; guests must bring their own wine. The inn is also a popular place for weddings.

The four guest rooms are all very large and beautifully appointed, with tall, wide windows that give each one an open, light feeling. When guests arrive, they find bouquets of fresh flowers, usually from the garden, in the rooms. The focal point of each room is the bed. One room has a high four-poster, an enormous mirrored armoire, and an antique trunk and love seat. Another has a bed with a high headboard, a marble-topped dresser, and a "mammy bench" with a seat for the mammy to rock the baby in the crib half of the bench. One room has two matching beds with high, carved headboards, another has a Marseille spread and a hand-knotted cover on the canopy. The two back rooms open onto the second-floor gallery.

The closets, unusual in a house of this age, were large enough to make into half baths that are shared between two rooms. Two striking full baths occupy the third floor, spectacular enough to make guests want to climb an extra flight of stairs. Beyond an etched-glass door, one bath is done in a masculine, rustic style with rough wood walls, a tin roof, and a zebra-skin bath mat in front of the old tin tub with copper rim and faux-marble sides. The marble washstand, however, is genuine and French. The second bath is decidedly feminine, with a mirrored wall and stained-glass skylight. The footed tub, satin-covered fainting couch, Swedish needlework screen, and crystal chandelier give the room an Empire touch.

THE HILL COUNTRY

FROM SAN ANTONIO NORTH TO LLANO

MARBLE FALLS

SALADO

GEORGETOWN

AUSTIN

BASTROP

SAN MARCOS

NEW BRAUNFELS

CASTROVILLE

CUERO

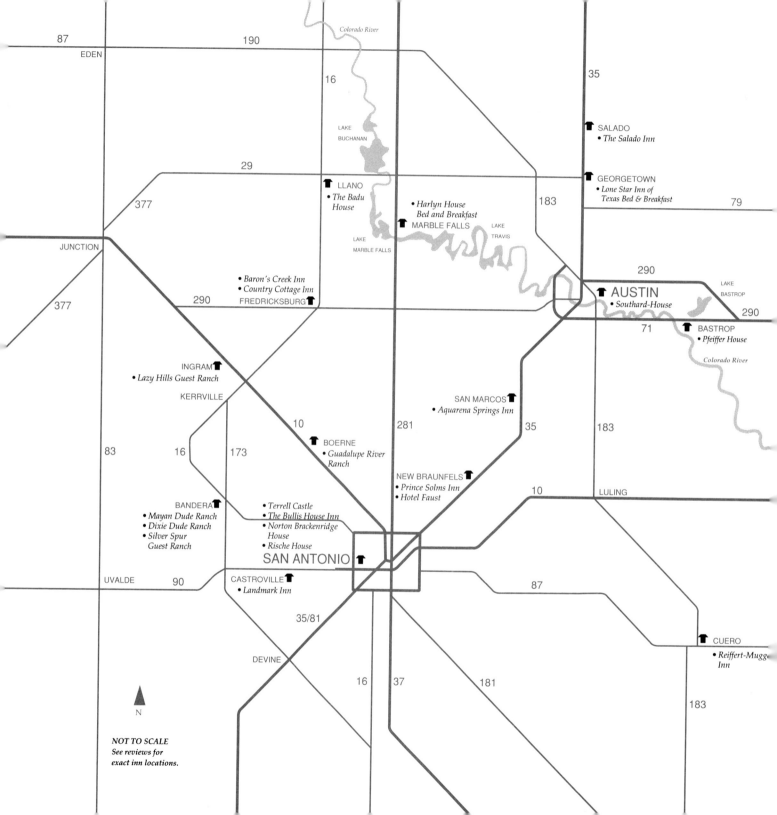

87 EDEN

190

Colorado River

16

LAKE BUCHANAN

35

🚩 SALADO
• *The Salado Inn*

29

377

🚩 LLANO
• *The Badu House*

• *Harlyn House Bed and Breakfast*
🚩 MARBLE FALLS

LAKE TRAVIS

🚩 GEORGETOWN
• *Lone Star Inn of Texas Bed & Breakfast*

183

79

JUNCTION

LAKE MARBLE FALLS

377

• *Baron's Creek Inn*
• *Country Cottage Inn*
290 FREDERICKSBURG 🚩

290

🚩 AUSTIN
• *Southard-House*

LAKE BASTROP

290

71 🚩 BASTROP
• *Pfeiffer House*

Colorado River

INGRAM 🚩
• *Lazy Hills Guest Ranch*

KERRVILLE

SAN MARCOS 🚩
• *Aquarena Springs Inn*

83

16

173

10

🚩 BOERNE
• *Guadalupe River Ranch*

281

35

183

BANDERA 🚩
• *Mayan Dude Ranch*
• *Dixie Dude Ranch*
• *Silver Spur Guest Ranch*

• *Terrell Castle*
• *The Bullis House Inn*
• *Norton Brackenridge House*
• *Rische House*

NEW BRAUNFELS 🚩
• *Prince Solms Inn*
• *Hotel Faust*

10 LULING

SAN ANTONIO 🚩

CASTROVILLE 🚩
• *Landmark Inn*

87

UVALDE 90

35/81

DEVINE

16

37

181

🚩 CUERO
• *Reiffert-Mugg Inn*

183

↑ N

NOT TO SCALE
See reviews for exact inn locations.

From the landing, another set of steps leads to the rooftop captain's walk, which offers a view of the surrounding horse country. Summer, when everything is in bloom, is the most beautiful time of year. Guests often sit on the gallery overlooking the gardens and listen to the wind chimes and the birds. The swimming pool is a few hundred yards from the house, and just beyond the trees is a miniature-gauge railroad, large enough to take guests on a spin around the tracks and past the replica of a Santa Fe station.

The station houses two less formal guest rooms decorated in a railroad motif, each with a private bath. A portable television is available on request, and a stay at the station house includes breakfast at the mansion.

Most things in the house are for sale and each room has a price sheet by the door. There is also an antiques shop in the weathered barn next to the main house.

Getting There: From Houston take Highway 290 to Chappell Hill. At the blinker light on the highway turn left and go two blocks. The road dead ends at a bar. Turn left and go about 100 feet to a gravel road. Make a sharp right; you'll see a sign for the inn, which is another quarter mile down the dirt road.

Hotels on this spot alongside the old Galveston, Harrisburg, and San Antonio railroad line have had a checkered history. The railroad came to Weimar in 1873. Two years later, the Jackson Hotel was built, but it burned in 1900; its replacement, the New Jackson Hotel, was destroyed by a hurricane nine years later. The third hotel on the site, built in 1909, was called the San Jacinto, and now houses the Weimar Country Inn.

Not much has changed in Weimar in the past eighty years. There are still about two thousand residents who hold tight to their European cultural traditions. In spring and fall, almost every little town in the area has a German festival or county fair. In the spring the wildflowers bloom; antiques shopping is a year-round attraction. Long country walks and bicycling are favorite activities for visitors, as is golf and tennis or croquet on the inn's lawn. There is even a historical square to explore just down the street from the inn.

The original twenty small rooms in the inn have been reduced to nine spacious rooms filled with country antiques and handmade quilts. The second story has the original peg-wood floors accented with braided rugs, and most of the rooms have wallpapers in keeping with the country flavor. Stained-glass transoms, each

WEIMAR COUNTRY INN
101 West Jackson,
Weimar, Texas 78962

Telephone: (409) 725-8888
or 725-9522

Accommodations: nine rooms with twin, queen-, or king-size beds; private and shared baths with tub/shower; telephones available; four rooms with television.

Rates: inexpensive to moderate, Continental breakfast included. Restaurant open for lunch and dinner Friday through Sunday. Children over five welcome. No pets.

Cards: AE, MC, V

Limited wheelchair access. Open all year.

reflecting the name of the room, were made for the hotel. And the rooms are decidedly patriotic as befits this hotel that stands on the Independence Trail, the route taken by Sam Houston and his army as they marched toward San Jacinto and Texas independence.

The San Jacinto has ruffled curtains, a brass bed, mirrored armoire, and braided rug. A Lone Star flag flies over the transom of the Texas Room. The Sam Houston has a handmade double wedding-ring quilt in shades of blue, and the Alamo is a corner room done in blues and yellow. Eight of the rooms have modern, private baths. Three can be closed off from the rest of the hotel and rented as a suite, with two shared baths down their own private hallway.

A Continental buffet breakfast of homemade cinnamon rolls, kolache, biscuits, and muffins is served on the second-floor landing.

The hotel is a far cry from the vehicle maintenance yard the building had been slated for. The city bought the property after the San Jacinto closed its doors in 1970 and auctioned off everything. What was left was vandalized. To save the old building Ron and Sara Jones bought and restored it.

One of their additions was the sun room that is now part of the restaurant. Here, big windows overlook the gardens and sunlight filters through ficus trees, lace curtains, and antique stained-glass "suncatchers."

The cowboy saloon is a typical Texas railroad-town bar, with a red pressed-tin ceiling and swinging doors. The ornate back bar is from Portugal and is part of an oversized buffet. Dominoes and checkers sit out waiting to be played. The only concessions to the twentieth century are the jukebox and the big-screen television. The hotel lobby is more formal, with an Oriental carpet and clusters of Victorian-style settees and wing chairs.

Getting There: From Houston, take Interstate 10 to Weimar. Take Highway 155 north to Highway 90. Turn left on 90, left again at the fourth stoplight, and go across the railroad tracks. Transportation available from municipal airport in La Grange.